CAMBRIDGE

EMPOWER
SECOND EDITION
WORKBOOK
WITH ANSWERS

C1
ADVANCED

Robert McLarty

CONTENTS

3

1A | I THOUGHT I COULD PICK UP ITALIAN BY EAR

1 GRAMMAR
Adverbs and adverbial phrases

a Complete the text with the words in the box.

clearly   apparently   effectively   widely
unfortunately   ~~simply~~   extremely

Whether you are a student, a professional athlete, an engineer or [1] _____simply_____ a tourist, English has become a(n) [2]_____ important skill to acquire. English will soon be the language of choice in most major fields of study, if it isn't already. Therefore, students embarking on their studies [3]_____ need to decide: what language do I want to get my degree in? Degrees in medicine delivered in English at a university in Poland are [4]_____ very popular, but you need a reasonable level of English to start. If you need to study English before university, it's [5]_____ agreed that you learn the most [6]_____ in an English-speaking environment. [7]_____, not all students can afford the time and cost of studying abroad.

b Put the words in the correct order to make sentences.

1 that hard / people think / isn't / Russian is / to learn / difficult, but it .
   People think Russian is difficult, but it isn't
   that hard to learn.

2 you listen / rapidly if / will improve / and watch films / to music / your English .
   _____
   _____

3 England / language schools / have opened / in the last ten years in / a lot of .
   _____
   _____

4 presumably / you lived / so / speak / you / fluently / Thai / in Bangkok, .
   _____
   _____

5 hardest / for / adult learners, / listening is / the / usually / skill .
   _____
   _____

6 never / vocabulary / new / I / down / write / almost .
   _____
   _____

2 VOCABULARY Language learning

a Underline the correct words to complete the sentences.

1 I studied Spanish at university, but I'm going to Valencia next year to *pick* / *brush* / *take* up on it.
2 My brother speaks four languages – he really has an *ear* / *eye* / *mouth* for them.
3 I know Japanese is hard, but you have to keep *on* / *to* / *at* it if you want the job.
4 I'm French, but my son was born in Italy. From an early age, he *pulled* / *picked* / *took* up a lot of Italian expressions.
5 I studied in China and I *fought* / *raced* / *struggled* with writing the characters for a long time.
6 It takes time to get *accustomed* / *ready* / *along* to a new teaching style.
7 My Turkish is a bit *cracked* / *broken* / *rusty*. I haven't spoken it for a while.
8 My sister can hold a *chat* / *speech* / *conversation* in several European languages.

3 VOCABULARY Noun forms

a Read the text and complete the words in the sentences below.

DEGREE IN MEDICINE

We run a complete five-year degree course in medicine, with all lectures and seminars delivered in English by our very competent and dedicated staff. Participants must have an excellent level of English and above all be highly motivated to be capable future doctors. Our course is very interactive and nearly all our candidates pass with good grades, despite living in Warsaw, where there are so many things to take your mind off studying. We have occasional misunderstandings when one language interferes with another, but generally the course runs well.

1 An advanced level of English is an absolute n<u>ecessity</u> on this course.
2 Our teachers show great d_____ to the course and the students.
3 M_____ is never a problem for our students, who all want to become doctors.
4 All our lectures have elements of i_____ to involve the students.
5 There are many d_____ in a city like Warsaw, so students have to stay focused.
6 Our students need both medical and linguistic c_____, which can be challenging.
7 Polish students may feel a r_____ to speak English if all their classmates speak Polish.
8 It is hard to avoid i_____ from the mother tongue, even if your English is excellent.

1B | LANGUAGE HAS BEEN CONSTANTLY EVOLVING

1 GRAMMAR The perfect aspect

a Underline the correct words to complete the sentences.

1 The team *had been training* / *has been training* for three months when the season started.
2 By September, I *will have been studying* / *will study* Arabic for three years.
3 I only joined the choir at university because I *haven't found* / *hadn't found* anything else to do.
4 This is the fourth time I *try* / *have tried* to learn to dance.
5 I *never have written* / *have never written* such a difficult essay as this one.
6 She *has been revising* / *had been revising* for this exam since early this morning.

b Complete the conversation using the correct form of the verb in brackets.

ROBERT	Thank you for coming, Sonia.
SONIA	My pleasure. Thank you for the opportunity.
ROBERT	So how long ¹ <u>have you been living</u> (live) in Brighton
SONIA	By December, I ²_____ (be) here for two years.
ROBERT	³_____ (you/ever/have) a job in the hotel industry before?
SONIA	Yes, I ⁴_____ . I worked in a hotel in Málaga for eighteen months before I moved here.
ROBERT	So why did you apply for this particular position?
SONIA	As soon as I saw it, I knew it was the right job for me.
ROBERT	What do you like about it?
SONIA	I ⁵_____ (always/enjoy) working with people and helping them, so this position seems ideal.
ROBERT	This isn't your first application, is it?
SONIA	No, this is the second time I ⁶_____ (apply). The first time my English wasn't good enough.
ROBERT	It sounds good now.
SONIA	It ⁷_____ (get) a lot better. I ⁸_____ (just/arrive) in Brighton the last time I applied.
ROBERT	Do you have any questions?
SONIA	When will I know if I ⁹_____ (get) the job?
ROBERT	We ¹⁰_____ (make) our decision by the end of next week. Ten days at the most.
SONIA	That sounds great. I look forward to hearing from you.

c ▶ **01.01** Listen and check.

2 VOCABULARY Describing changes

a Complete the text with the words in the box.

rapid   changes   substantially   ~~noticeable~~   way
barely   shift   increase   subtle   ongoing

Changes to the English language may not always be immediately ¹ <u>noticeable</u>, but because over 500 million people now use it as their first language, it is constantly evolving.

Some ²_____ changes, often made in an attempt to simplify the language, are ³_____ perceptible. However, over time we notice that people are not using 'ought to' as much any more, and 'right?' is being used instead of question tags, which seem to be on the ⁴_____ out.

The use of Americanisms by British youth is clearly on the ⁵_____, with expressions such as, 'Can I get a coffee to go?' becoming very common. Interest in American TV programmes and music has grown ⁶_____ over the last 20 years, leading to a ⁷_____ rise in American usage.

Linguists and lexicographers spot the most ⁸_____ changes in the language and make decisions as to whether a steady ⁹_____ over time is enough to justify a new dictionary entry or even a change to a grammar rule.

The most lasting ¹⁰_____ to the language come as the result of major innovations in lifestyle. The digital revolution, just like the automotive revolution a hundred years before, has introduced a large number of new expressions and usages, from 'selfie' to 'tweet' to 'microblogging.'

3 PRONUNCIATION Sentence stress

a ▶ **01.02** Listen and underline the stressed words in **bold**.

1 The team **had been <u>training</u>** for three months already when the season started.
2 By September, I **will have been studying** Arabic for three years.
3 This is the fourth time I **have tried** to learn ballroom dancing.
4 They **have been practising** this piece on the piano for about three months now.
5 By the time I got to rehearsal, the actors **had been working** for about an hour.
6 She **has been revising** for this exam since early this morning.

1C EVERYDAY ENGLISH
Something along those lines

1 USEFUL LANGUAGE
Expressing yourself in an inexact way

a Complete the conversation with the expressions in the box.

loads of   give or take   something to do with
words to that effect   ~~sort of~~   whatshisname
somewhere in the region of

TIM	Thanks for helping me with this, Harry. I really appreciate it.
HARRY	No problem, Tim.
TIM	This is ¹___sort of___ my first report and I want to get it right.
HARRY	Sure. I still remember my first one.
TIM	You've done ²_____ them since then, I suppose. How long have you been here?
HARRY	Twenty years. ³_____ a couple.
TIM	So you've done a lot of reports?
HARRY	Quite a few.
TIM	Hundreds, I expect. So, who should I copy my report to?
HARRY	⁴_____ in Finance and probably that other guy.
TIM	Who?
HARRY	Thingy. The tall guy. He's ⁵_____ sales. It'll come back to me. Next question?
TIM	How long should the report be?
HARRY	Not too long.
TIM	Quite short then? Good.
HARRY	But not too short. ⁶_____ three or four pages.
TIM	That's not too hard then. Three to four pages. Plus a cover page. What should I call it?
HARRY	*The future of the company.* Or ⁷_____.
TIM	Brilliant idea. Final question. Can I buy you lunch?
HARRY	Of course you can. What's the budget?
TIM	About a tenner. Will that be enough?
HARRY	I suppose it'll have to be. Let's go.

b ▶01.03 Listen and check.

c Match questions 1–6 with responses a–f.

1 [e] Who lent you this book?
2 [ ] Can I borrow one of these pencils?
3 [ ] Did he say I wasn't invited to the wedding?
4 [ ] What was that phone call about?
5 [ ] What's quinoa?
6 [ ] How much are the flights?

a Something to do with our Internet connection.
b Well, words to that effect.
c They're somewhere in the region of £500 per person.
d Sure! I've got loads of them!
e Oh, whatshername, the girl with the red hair.
f It's a sort of cereal. It's a bit like rice.

2 PRONUNCIATION
Sound and spelling: *ea*, *ee* and *ie*

a ▶01.04 Listen. How are the letters in **bold** pronounced in each word? Complete the table.

1 It's a good car**ee**r.
2 I prefer the gr**ee**n one.
3 Let's have fruit inst**ea**d.
4 I never w**ea**r a tie.
5 People don't **ea**rn much here.
6 Shall we have a br**ea**k?
7 I don't bel**ie**ve it.
8 I can't b**ea**r it.
9 I'm going to the p**ie**r.
10 What did you l**ea**rn?
11 He's a gr**ea**t player.
12 Br**ea**d, anyone?

Sound 1 /iː/ (e.g. *be*)	Sound 2 /e/ (e.g. *ten*)	Sound 3 /eɪ/ (e.g. *take*)
Sound 4 /eə/ (e.g. *hair*)	**Sound 5 /ɪə/** (e.g. *hear*)	**Sound 6 /ɜː/** (e.g. *serve*)
	career	

1D | SKILLS FOR WRITING
You're spot on there!

1 READING

a Read the blog. Are the sentences true or false?

1 Takahiro likes Edinburgh.
2 Takahiro thinks the food is not strongly flavoured.
3 Takahiro is the last person to come home every day.
4 Takahiro has the same classes five days a week.
5 Takahiro has an active social life.
6 Takahiro is thinking a lot about the weather in Japan.

b Takahiro's blog started a heated discussion on the value of studying English abroad. Read some opinions (1–8) that were expressed in the comments. Are the opinions direct or softened? Tick (✓) the correct box.

		Direct	Softened
1	How can you possibly think that?	✓	☐
2	That doesn't make sense, if you ask me.	☐	☐
3	I don't get what all the fuss is about.	☐	☐
4	I have to say, I'm in two minds about this.	☐	☐
5	It seems to me you are missing the point.	☐	☐
6	No way!	☐	☐
7	That's rubbish.	☐	☐
8	I'm sorry, but that simply isn't true.	☐	☐

2 WRITING SKILLS Expressing opinions

a Correct the wrong words in each sentence.

1 Sorry, but that's the load of rubbish.
  Sorry, but that's a load of rubbish.

2 I disagree. However, you've got the point about the price of transport.

3 I'm in two heads about this. I'm not sure if you are right or not.

4 I don't really guess what the fuss is about. In my opinion, Edinburgh is cheap.

5 You're on spot there! Listening is really tricky. Keep practising.

6 I agree with the others to a point, but I think speaking is harder. Good luck!

7 You are all missing the points. Learning English just takes time.

8 I had go along with that. Good discussion, by the way.

First Impressions – Takahiro Yoshida

I've already been here for one week and I must say my first impressions of Edinburgh are very positive. All the international students are staying with families for the first two weeks, and then we move into our own accommodation for two more months.

I think I've been very lucky – my room is nice and large, just a bit dark, and the food is generally excellent, if a bit plain. The family, particularly the children, are very friendly and patient with my English. The father works until quite late, but the mother and children always have dinner with me.

The city seems less busy than Kyoto, and the bus system seems to be very efficient, if a little expensive. We have English classes every morning and we have afternoon lectures three times a week. The lecturers speak quite quickly – I hope my listening improves soon. We have a lot of homework every night and there is always one exercise I have to discuss with my family, which gives us an opportunity to talk.

I have visited the castle and one of the museums this week and I went with my friends to a concert. It was very busy and noisy. Overall, I am very happy here and am looking forward to the next two months. The thing I miss most is rice and miso soup!

3 WRITING

a Read the post on a web forum. Write a comment of five or six sentences giving your point of view. Remember to express your opinions clearly and support your ideas.

IN THE FUTURE, WE WON'T NEED TEACHERS

Over the last 20 years, the Internet has developed to such a degree that soon most subjects we want to study will be available to us online. We can already attend MOOCs and watch videos of lectures taking place at some of the most prestigious universities in the world. We can do the follow-up reading and listen to the lecture as many times as we want. All of this is available 24 hours a day and it's free of charge.

We can also access micro-teaching, where short clips and texts are posted online. These small chunks of information allow us to learn at our own pace at a rate we can cope with. Most Internet pages are also translated these days, so if we want to compare a text in two languages, we can. Likewise, if we want a video to be subtitled, that is often possible, too.

With all this information continuously available free of charge, it will be easier for all of us to learn online. This is particularly useful for people in remote regions who cannot attend schools or universities or for people who for other reasons cannot travel for their education.

The idea of lifelong learning is that we never stop developing and learning new content and skills. Thanks to the Internet, we can still grow and learn without a formal classroom.

Like · Comment · Share   27   9

COMMENTS

1 READING

a Read the article. Match paragraphs 1–6 with summaries a–f.

a ☐ Challenges for language teachers
b ☐ Ways of making CLIL successful
c ☐1 Introducing the subject
d ☐ Challenges for subject teachers
e ☐ Whether or not CLIL works
f ☐ A reason for CLIL

b Underline the best words to complete the sentences.

1 The idea of studying subjects and languages together can make both students and teachers *enthusiastic* / *anxious* / *excited*.
2 The European Union wants its citizens to *speak several languages* / *improve their English* / *become more efficient*.
3 CLIL classes *are based on* / *try to follow* / *do not follow* the traditional structure of language classes.
4 In CLIL, grammatical structures *are more important than* / *come out of* / *are learned separately from* the subject information being taught.
5 The idea behind CLIL has existed *for a short time* / *for hundreds of years* / *since the 1990s*.

c According to the article, are the sentences true or false, or is there not enough information to be sure?

1 The CLIL method is used in many places.
2 Using CLIL means that schools save lesson time.
3 CLIL materials are designed to present language structures in a logical order.
4 Students learn grammar better in CLIL classes.
5 Subject teachers usually have language classes before teaching CLIL.
6 When content and language teachers teach CLIL, they both have to change their style.
7 CLIL only works with highly able students.
8 CLIL students end up with better language skills than students taught traditionally.

d Write a short essay giving your reactions to the idea of CLIL. Include answers to these questions:

- Do you have CLIL lessons or do you think you would enjoy them?
- What are the advantages?
- What are the disadvantages?
- What are the practical implications for teachers and students?
- Do you think CLIL should be introduced in primary schools? Secondary schools? Give your reasons.

Could you learn physics in Japanese?

1 Learning a language is hard enough, as is learning a subject like maths or physics. But doing both things simultaneously in the same class? It may sound daunting, but that's precisely the approach taken in the now-widespread methodology known as CLIL (Content and Language Integrated Learning).

2 CLIL was introduced in Europe in the 1990s, primarily to meet the European Union aims of producing multilingual populations. One of its main justifications was efficiency; if languages could be picked up through exposure to other subjects, pressure on packed timetables would be reduced.

3 Of course, CLIL brings many challenges, especially for teachers who are required to make radical adjustments to the way they teach. For language teachers, there is a near-complete reversal of what they are accustomed to: whereas in a traditional language class, texts are constructed primarily as a vehicle for the language points they want to teach, in CLIL the language emerges somewhat randomly from the subject content. With grammar, for example, there is much less opportunity to focus on specific points, but the theory is that students learn appropriate use through the context in which they come across the language.

4 Conversely, subject teachers can no longer talk about their subjects to their students and assume they will understand everything. They will almost certainly need to adopt some different approaches, such as greater levels of practical demonstration or experimentation, rather than relying so heavily on language to convey information. There is also a good deal of fear to overcome. Subject teachers may have attained only low levels of language skills and therefore lack confidence in teaching in a foreign language, while a language teacher's initial reaction to the idea of teaching maths will often be one of horror!

5 Solutions to these problems will vary according to the setting in which teachers work. Good CLIL teaching materials are increasingly available, while many schools practise a collaborative approach, with language and subject teachers negotiating both the balance between language and content and the ways in which their different teaching styles can be brought together in a successful lesson.

6 So does CLIL work? Well, as with many so-called innovations, the basic theory behind CLIL has been around for centuries, with even upper-middle class Ancient Romans preferring their offspring to be educated in Greek. Ideas don't tend to persist if they have no value, and now that many schools have been implementing CLIL for a number of years, research seems to indicate that it has been producing good results with mixed-ability classes as well as elite students. It could be that the concentration required to understand the language means that the subject information is correspondingly well absorbed.

2 LISTENING

a ▶ 01.05 Listen to the conversation between Zac and Rebecca. Tick (✓) the best summary.

1 ☐ Zac and Rebecca talk about changes to the grammar and vocabulary of the English language. Rebecca gives Zac some examples of new words and Zac is very surprised.

2 ☐ Zac and Rebecca discuss words that have recently come into English. David doesn't think that any new words should be put into the dictionary.

3 ☐ Zac and Rebecca talk about new words. Rebecca explains where some new words come from. Zac has strong opinions about some of them.

b ▶ 01.05 Listen again. Who expresses opinions 1–10: Zac, Rebecca or neither of them?

1 It is surprising to hear that we need new dictionaries.
2 New dictionaries are needed to record language change.
3 Every dictionary should have at least 200 words added every year.
4 Words like 'Zoombombing' shouldn't be in dictionaries.
5 Lexicographers leave out words they consider too informal.
6 Some words are popular for a short time and then die out.
7 Technology words come and go because technology itself changes quickly.
8 Many new words come from other languages.
9 Portmanteau words are common in fashion.
10 The subject of food produces more words than any other.

c Write a conversation between two friends about changes to your first language. Think about these questions or use ideas of your own:

• Has your language changed much recently?
• Can you think of any new words in your language and, if so, what subject areas do they come from?
• Is there a national organisation in your country that 'protects' your language?
• Have words from other languages come into your language?
• Do you approve or disapprove of changes to your language?

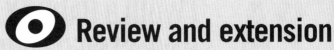

👁 Review and extension

1 GRAMMAR AND VOCABULARY

Correct the errors in the underlined words.

1 I watch the news and I like especially films.
 I watch the news and I especially like films.
2 They were hoping really to stay with us, but nobody told us.
3 She speaks fluent Italian and she knows also Turkish.
4 You can find easily a shop which sells fruit and vegetables.
5 I met the teacher recently who taught me history at school.
6 As the restaurant grew in popularity, we felt the necessary to take on more staff.
7 We concluded that the program had some serious limitation.
8 The improvement in performance was most noticable in the second half of the year.
9 The number of days off taken by employees increased steady throughout November and December.
10 We received a substancial increase in funding from one of our benefactors.

2 WORDPOWER Idioms: Body parts

Rewrite the sentences. Replace the underlined words with the words in the box. Make any changes needed.

fight tooth and nail   ~~head and shoulders above~~
a safe pair of hands   bite one's tongue
have a nose for

1 Our local beach volleyball team is brilliant – so much better than the other teams in the area.
 Our local beach volleyball team is brilliant – head and shoulders above the other teams in the area.
2 She can be very rude – I have to stop myself from saying something to her to avoid an argument.
3 When I was a child, my mother tried very hard to get me the best education possible, and she succeeded!
4 I love going shopping with my friend Sandra – she's really good at finding bargains!
5 I recently employed an accountant to manage my money. I'm so glad I did – he's doing a great job.

🔄 REVIEW YOUR PROGRESS

Look again at Review your progress on p. 18 of the Student's Book. How well can you do these things now?
3 = very well   2 = well   1 = not so well

I CAN ...	
talk about learning a second language	☐
describe languages and how they change	☐
express myself in an inexact way	☐
write a web forum post.	☐

2A | I WOULD HAPPILY HAVE STAYED LONGER

1 GRAMMAR Comparison

a Underline the correct words to complete the text.

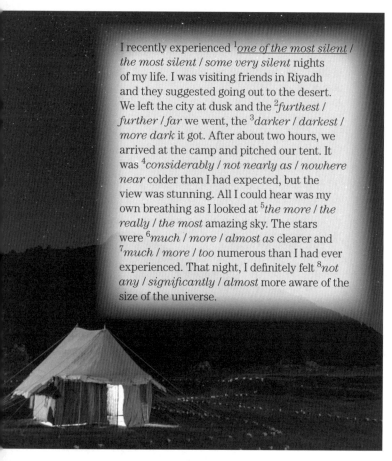

I recently experienced [1]*one of the most silent / the most silent / some very silent* nights of my life. I was visiting friends in Riyadh and they suggested going out to the desert. We left the city at dusk and the [2]*furthest / further / far* we went, the [3]*darker / darkest / more dark* it got. After about two hours, we arrived at the camp and pitched our tent. It was [4]*considerably / not nearly as / nowhere near* colder than I had expected, but the view was stunning. All I could hear was my own breathing as I looked at [5]*the more / the really / the most* amazing sky. The stars were [6]*much / more / almost as* clearer and [7]*much / more / too* numerous than I had ever experienced. That night, I definitely felt [8]*not any / significantly / almost* more aware of the size of the universe.

b ▶ 02.01 Listen and check.

2 VOCABULARY
Multi-word verbs: social interaction

a Match the expressions in **bold** in 1–8 with the definitions a–h.

1. [c] She doesn't **come across** very **well**.
2. [ ] She **complains about** her ex-boss.
3. [ ] She **cuts herself off** from some of us.
4. [ ] She's always **running down** her colleagues.
5. [ ] She **bombards** her team **with questions**.
6. [ ] She **doesn't really fit in** here.
7. [ ] She never **holds back** in meetings.
8. [ ] She **brings out the worst** in me.

a stop oneself from saying something
b ask too many questions
c make a good impression
d ignore completely
e be different from everyone else
f be very critical
g make other people act badly
h say something or someone is wrong or not good enough

b Underline the correct words to complete the conversation.

A So, tell me all. How was the big meeting?
B It was a bit more relaxed than I'd expected.
A So did you manage to [1]*bring / fit / get* in with all those important people?
B I guess so. I hope I [2]*went / brought / came* across well – there were a number of people I could [3]*like / relate / take* to.
A How was the 'Big Boss'?
B He was OK. When I first got there, he [4]*asked / discussed / bombarded* me with questions about our current project. Overall, I think I did quite well, actually. Mind you, my thoughts on the manager nearly [5]*left / brought / slipped* out.
A I hope you [6]*held / got / saw* yourself back.
B Of course I did. Some of the discussions [7]*took / showed / brought* out the worst in some of the participants. One man [8]*said / went on and on / told* about the budget. It was as if he was the only one affected. Anyway, the whole thing was fine. It was a great day, and I learned lots.
A Well done! You obviously handled the whole thing very professionally.

c ▶ 02.02 Listen and check.

3 PRONUNCIATION
Consonant-vowel linking

a ▶ 02.03 Listen to the sentences and mark the consonant–vowel linking with the symbol ‿.

1 It was‿a bit more relaxed than‿I'd‿expected.
2 So did you manage to fit in with all those important people?
3 Overall, I think I did quite well, actually.
4 One man went on and on about the budget.
5 It was a great day and I learned lots.

2B | I'LL BE JUMPING FROM 900 METRES

1 GRAMMAR
Intentions and arrangements

a Complete the email using the phrases in the box.

> is due to   ~~are leaving~~   hoping to   arrive on
> about to   won't see   plan to take her   will be
> will be going   are thinking of

Dear Kenzo,

Just a quick email to tell you about our trip to Australia.
We [1] _are leaving_ this Friday, initially for Adelaide,
because Sarah is graduating. We [2]_____
Saturday at eleven and the ceremony is that afternoon
at three!

She's [3]_____ stay in Adelaide and study for a
Master's degree, so it [4]_____ good to see her for
a few days. She [5]_____ find out next week, so
she will know soon enough if she's staying in Adelaide.
If she gets accepted, we [6]_____ on a short
trip because we [7]_____ her again for at least
six months.

After that, we fly to Queensland, so it would be great to
meet up. I'm not sure if you [8]_____ to the NCON
conference in Brisbane. We'll be there on the 22nd
and 23rd. I'm giving a presentation on the 23rd. We
[9]_____ seeing Antonia on the evening of the
22nd — she is supposed to confirm by Friday. Anyway, if
you are going to be there, let's meet up. We're not going
to visit Victoria this time.

That's all for now, I have a call that is [10]_____
start.

Regards,

Tom

b Read the email again. Complete the table with the events in the box.

> ~~Tom's trip to Australia~~   Tom's presentation
> meeting with Kenzo   trip to Victoria   trip with Sarah
> Kenzo attending conference   Sarah's graduation
> dinner with Antonia   Tom's call

Definite	Definitely not	Possible
Tom's trip to Australia		

2 VOCABULARY Verbs of movement

a Complete the crossword puzzle.

→ Across
3 move very quickly, especially in a way that seems dangerous
5 move slowly, often on hands and knees
6 walk unsteadily as if about to fall
7 walk slowly and with difficulty because of an injured or painful leg or foot

↓ Down
1 move suddenly forwards or downwards
2 rise into the air very quickly
4 move easily over a wet or slippery surface
5 walk very quietly to avoid being seen or heard

b Complete the sentences with the words in the box.

> drifting   strolling   marched
> rushed   ~~hurtling~~   zoomed

1 I love the feeling of ___hurtling___ downhill on my skis.
2 The protestors _____ towards the headquarters, gathering support as they went.
3 I was driving home today when suddenly a motorbike _____ past me at about 150 kph.
4 With the anchor raised, the boat started _____ slowly downstream.
5 Having overslept, he _____ out of the house so he wouldn't miss the train.
6 You can't beat the feeling of _____ in the sunshine without a care in the world.

2C EVERYDAY ENGLISH
Don't get so wound up about it

1 USEFUL LANGUAGE Giving advice

a Complete the conversation with appropriate words.

MARCO What's the problem, Luisa?

LUISA Nothing major. Well, actually … Don't you dare tell anyone, but I'm thinking of leaving.

MARCO You? Quitting? Why?

LUISA My job is quite dull and the manager doesn't seem to realise I'm bored.

MARCO Have you told him?

LUISA Indirectly. I've dropped lots of hints.

MARCO Yes, but there's a lot to be [1] _____said_____ for being upfront. You need to tell him directly.

LUISA He won't listen.

MARCO It might even be in your [2] _____ to go above him and talk to his manager. It's [3] _____ time you sorted this problem out.

LUISA I don't think I could do that, Marco. That's not really my style. I just need a new challenge and I don't think I'm going to get it here and that's that.

MARCO Don't [4] _____ so defensive about it. Why don't you speak to HR?

LUISA There's no point.

MARCO I disagree. You might [5] _____ to try this. Have you thought about the [6] _____ of asking for a secondment or even a sabbatical?

LUISA A sabbatical? That's not a bad idea. OK, I'll give it some thought.

b ▶ 02.04 Listen and check.

c Match sentences 1–5 with responses a–e.

1 [a] Why don't you come with me?
2 [ ] There's a lot to be said for cycling to work.
3 [ ] You might want to read this.
4 [ ] It's about time you went home.
5 [ ] You might as well cancel the meeting.

a I am sure you'll be fine on your own.
b Why? How many can't come?
c I will as soon as I've finished this.
d Really? What's it about?
e I agree. Cheaper and healthier.

d ▶ 02.05 Listen and check.

2 PRONUNCIATION Emphatic stress

a ▶ 02.06 Listen and underline the stressed word in the responses.

1 **A** Did the manager email the supplier last week?
B No, she telephoned them last week.
2 **A** Did the manager email the supplier last week?
B No, she emailed them last month.
3 **A** Did all the participants speak English during the meeting?
B No, everyone spoke German during the meeting.
4 **A** Did all the participants speak English during the meeting?
B No, but the presenters spoke English.
5 **A** Will you be going to Italy on holiday again this year?
B No, but I'll be going there for work.
6 **A** Will you be going to Italy on holiday again this year?
B No, I think we'll be going to Greece.
7 **A** Are you flying to the meeting in Paris next week?
B No, I think I'll be driving there.
8 **A** So you are doing a presentation in Berlin?
B No, I'm doing a workshop in Berlin.

SKILLS FOR WRITING
Less adventurous students could try paintball

1 READING

a Read the report. Tick (✓) the questions that are answered in the text.

1 ✓ How long was the programme?
2 ☐ Where did the students study?
3 ☐ Did they take a direct flight?
4 ☐ What was the weather like during the first week?
5 ☐ Why did the students like the excursions?
6 ☐ How many teachers accompanied the group?

b Read the report again. Tick (✓) the correct words and phrases to complete the sentences.

1 The report is based on feedback from _____ sources.
   a ☐ one   b ☐ two   c ✓ four

2 It includes ideas to make the programme _____ next year.
   a ☐ longer   b ☐ better   c ☐ cheaper

3 The writer thinks it is worth paying for _____ next time.
   a ☐ direct flights
   b ☐ single rooms
   c ☐ better food

4 The classes had _____.
   a ☐ a mix of teachers
   b ☐ two teachers
   c ☐ one teacher

5 Of the activities mentioned, only the _____ did not take place.
   a ☐ excursions
   b ☐ tango dancing lessons
   c ☐ boat trip

6 The writer is keen to make the trip again _____.
   a ☐ only if there are two teachers
   b ☐ even if there is only one teacher
   c ☐ provided all the changes are made

2 WRITING SKILLS Reports; Linking: contrast and concession

a Complete the comments with the words in the box.

on the other hand   even though   unlike
alternatively   by comparison   ~~despite~~

1 I thoroughly enjoyed the trip, _despite_ the fact that there were four people in our room!
2 _____ I felt very shy at first, I still managed to make friends.
3 I didn't really enjoy Jack's classes. _____, I did learn a lot.
4 Our room was very small, _____ some of the girls' bedrooms.
5 Winters at home are cold but, _____, winter in Canada is freezing!
6 We should change teachers after the morning break or, _____, after lunch.

Report by teacher following overseas study programme

The purpose of this report is to review the overseas study programme this year. It is based on feedback from the travel agency, the teachers, the students themselves and my personal observations throughout the two-week period. Overall, I feel the programme was a success, but I would like to make a number of suggestions so that future trips are even more beneficial to the students.

In terms of the travel, the students were happy and well-behaved, although I would recommend a direct flight next time, even if it proves more expensive. Five hours at São Paulo airport is a long time to wait, particularly on the return journey. As far as the accommodation is concerned, students were generally positive, despite the fact that some of them were sleeping four to a room. On the other hand, everyone was unanimous in their praise for the food.

Generally, the lessons were viewed as challenging and varied. However, a number of students in the advanced class thought the teacher was not very dynamic and I think this should be noted for next year. One suggestion was for all the groups to have a mix of teachers. Alternatively, teachers could swap over in the second week.

Despite the bad weather in the second week, the recreational activities received great praise, in particular the two trips to Iguazu Falls and the tango dancing lessons. The only negative point was the cancellation of the boat trip.

In conclusion, I would say that the programme was a great success and, for next year, we should make the changes suggested above to make it an even better experience. I would also add that it would have been easier for me if the budget had allowed for a second teacher to accompany the group. Nevertheless, I would be delighted to be considered for next year's programme. I have attached some extracts from the survey I gave to the students to get their comments.

3 WRITING

a Write a short report (200 words) on the topic 'Something in your area that you feel could be improved'. Remember to use linkers to connect your ideas. Use these notes to help you:

- Introduce the problem. Where? What? Why?
- Describe your possible improvements. What? Why? How?
- What are the advantages and disadvantages of your suggestions?

1 READING

a Read the article about sensory play. Tick (✓) the best definition of *sensory play*.

1 ☐ play that involves making a mess with substances such as sand and water
2 ☐ play that involves experimenting and learning
3 ☐ play that involves using sight, smell, taste, touch and hearing

b Read the text again. Tick (✓) the correct answer.

1 Why is it clear that children enjoy sensory play?
  a ☐ Psychologists have proved it.
  b ☐ They have always done it.
  c ☑ We can see them doing it.

2 Why are new babies able to recognise their own mother's voice?
  a ☐ It's the first voice they hear when they are born.
  b ☐ They already understand that everyone's voice is different.
  c ☐ They've heard their mother's voice since before they were born.

3 Why do some people teach their babies sign language?
  a ☐ Sign language helps babies communicate their feelings without speech.
  b ☐ Babies can't speak if they are too upset.
  c ☐ It is important to deal with a baby's problems quickly.

4 Why does sensory play help children understand the physical world?
  a ☐ They directly experience the qualities of objects and substances.
  b ☐ They are given more educational toys to play with.
  c ☐ It will help them learn science in the future.

5 How can a parent bring language development into sensory play?
  a ☐ listening to children describe their experiences
  b ☐ describing the sensory experiences that are occurring
  c ☐ allowing children to make a mess

c Read the article again. Tick (✓) the opinions the author expresses.

1 ☐ The author thinks that young children are often reluctant to engage in sensory play.
2 ☐ She is rather surprised that babies are born with several sensory skills.
3 ☐ She is not completely convinced by the claims made about baby sign language.
4 ☐ She thinks that adults accept new ideas more easily than young children.
5 ☐ She thinks it's wrong for parents to keep their children too clean and neat.

d Imagine you are planning a lesson for a group of five-year-old children. You want to teach them about different substances, such as rubber, water, sand, wool and wood. Write two or three paragraphs. Remember to include:

• which senses will help the children learn about the substances
• what equipment you'll need
• what the children might learn during your lesson

NOISY, MESSY, slippery, sticky;

It's all good for your child!

Nobody who has witnessed a young child splashing in the bath or reaching out to grab a bunch of shiny keys will be in any doubt that kids love to use their senses, and they do so without any inhibitions! But it's not just about having fun. Sensory play is a vital part of a child's physical and psychological development, contributing to a range of skills such as hand–eye coordination, concentration and decision-making.

Even the sensory skills of newborn babies are nowhere near as undeveloped as we might imagine. Although their sight is not good, we know that they are comforted by the feeling of being cuddled and rocked, and they also exhibit marked reactions to music or strong smells. In addition, they will already have begun to hear sounds while still in the womb and – incredibly – are able to distinguish their mother's voice from other voices at birth.

Their sensory reactions also cause them to exhibit displeasure, such as at the feel of a wet nappy against their skin, or the unfamiliar texture of a new kind of food. Failure to recognise the cause of the ensuing screaming can be extremely frustrating for the parent or carer, as well as the child. That is why more and more parents are turning to a form of 'baby sign language,' which can be taught from the age of six months. Not only, say its advocates, does it eliminate the need for guesswork when your baby is awake and crying at 3 am but it also leads to higher educational attainment in later life.

Whether or not that is true, psychologists agree that, in general, sensory play is of great educational value to children, who are usually considerably more open to new ideas than their parents. As they pour sand from one container to another or plunge their hands into a bowl of dried beans, they are learning to relate to the world around them. Their play area becomes, in effect, a hands-on science lab where they can experiment, make predictions ('What will happen if I drop this egg on the floor?'), try out new concepts, and respond to their findings.

Sensory play can also help with language acquisition, particularly if the parent articulates what is going on: 'Can you feel the fur? Mmm, smell this soap.' And of course, from the moment children begin to speak, they bombard their parents with questions, all of which contribute to their speech and learning.

It's obvious that children enjoy using their senses, and all the evidence points to the fact that we should allow them the freedom to do so. Sand, mud, water; think of them as educational tools: the messier the better!

2 LISTENING

a ▶ 02.07 Listen to the conversation between Carla and Rakesh. Complete the sentences.

1 Rakesh has lost his sense of _____.
2 This also affects his sense of _____.
3 Carla's _____ had the same problem.
4 Rakesh's _____ isn't sure of the cause.

b ▶ 02.07 Listen again. Underline the correct words to complete the sentences.

1 Food *is* / *isn't* important to Rakesh.
2 Rakesh's girlfriend *is* / *isn't* sympathetic about his problem.
3 Carla *does* / *doesn't* understand Rakesh's problem.
4 Carla's uncle *did* / *didn't* make a full recovery from his stroke.
5 Rakesh *is* / *isn't* aware of the safety measures he needs to take.
6 Rakesh *has* / *hasn't* seen a specialist.
7 Rakesh's own doctor *knows* / *doesn't know* the reason for his problem.
8 Rakesh *thinks* / *doesn't think* that eating more healthily will help him with his problem.

c Which of these things are mentioned in the conversation? Tick (✓) the correct boxes.

1 Causes of loss of smell
  a ☐ stroke
  b ☐ reaction to medicine
  c ☐ head injury
  d ☐ blockage in the nose
  e ☐ infection from a virus
  f ☐ problems with nerve signals

2 Safety measures
  a ☐ smoke alarms
  b ☐ gas detector
  c ☐ checking chemicals such as household cleaners
  d ☐ checking dates on food

d Write a conversation between two people discussing the loss of one of their senses: taste, smell, sight, touch or hearing. Think about these questions or use ideas of your own:

• What would be the hardest sense to lose?
• What would be the physical and psychological consequences of losing a sense?
• What measures would someone need to take if they lost a sense?

 # Review and extension

1 GRAMMAR AND VOCABULARY

Correct the errors in the underlined words.

1 <u>More you work, you have more stress</u>.
  The more you work, the more stress you have.
2 I really hope you enjoy your course <u>so much as</u> I did.
3 Because I liked these friends, <u>I was more and more hanging around with them</u>.
4 Cars present a great danger for the environment, which is being polluted <u>quicker and quicker</u>.
5 I like the kitchen best because it is the room with <u>more light</u> and it has a nice atmosphere.
6 I'm glad to hear from you. <u>I'm trying to explain</u> everything about this job tomorrow when we speak.
7 I <u>lept</u> out of bed, put some clothes on and went down to the garage to my car.
8 One night we <u>crepted</u> into the office and borrowed the keys to the SUV!
9 I <u>slided</u> along the ice on my stomach to try to pull him out.
10 They were constantly <u>bombing</u> me with questions.

2 WORDPOWER Idioms: Movement

Rewrite the sentences. Replace the underlined words with the words in the box. Make any changes needed.

give it a whirl   feel a rush   ~~on a roll~~
jump at the chance   take the plunge

1 My cousin's a singer and she's <u>doing really well</u> at the moment – she won two singing competitions last month!
  My cousin's a singer and she's on a roll at the moment – she won two singing competitions last month!
2 A friend of mine has just turned down the chance to go on a three-week safari! I would <u>love</u> to have a holiday like that!
3 When I saw my favourite band on stage for the first time, I <u>got such a strong feeling</u> of excitement!
4 I never thought I'd get married, but last week I decided to <u>face my fear</u> and propose to Evelyn. She said yes!
5 There's a nice tapas restaurant nearby – I've never had tapas before, but it looks good, so I don't mind <u>trying it</u>.

↻ REVIEW YOUR PROGRESS

Look again at Review your progress on p. 30 of the Student's Book. How well can you do these things now?
3 = very well   2 = well   1 = not so well

I CAN ...	
describe extreme sensory experiences	☐
talk about plans, intentions and arrangements	☐
give advice	☐
write a report.	☐

3A | NEVER HAVE I HAD SUCH A REWARDING EXPERIENCE

1 GRAMMAR Inversion

a <u>Underline</u> the correct words to complete the text.

Mary's Meals is a charity providing food to over one million schoolchildren in developing countries, but ¹<u>not only</u> / no sooner does the nutritious meal fill their stomachs, it is also a motivation to attend school in the first place.

²It is rare / Seldom has a single charity done so much to help so many people. The teachers themselves are amazed at the difference in their students: ³'Never / Often have I felt and seen such a change in my students. They used to be so tired and hungry they found it impossible to learn, yet not once ⁴I heard them / did I hear them complain. Not until they started having a hot lunch every day ⁵did they start / they began to be lively and eager to contribute and participate in class,' says one elementary schoolteacher.

The projects continue to grow. ⁶'As soon as / No sooner has one project been set up than we are asked to do something in a neighbouring village or town,' comments one of the volunteers.

The food is sourced locally and cooked by volunteers, often relatives of the children. 'Not in a thousand years ⁷I would think / did I ever think a meal a day could change the lives of these kids so much, but not until every child has a meal every day ⁸can we really stop / we will never stop our work,' another volunteer adds.

b Put the words in the correct order to make comments by volunteers.

1 at no time / my old life in the UK / did I miss .
   <u>At no time did I miss my old life in the UK.</u>

2 a difference / feel / making / did I / I wasn't / not once .

3 kids learn to read / arrived in Bogotá / had / were helping / we / no sooner / than we .

4 also made / help a lot of / people, / we / we / did / great friends / not only .

5 will / ever forget / I / no way / things I saw there / the .

6 really help / chance to / we / people / do / rarely / get a .

2 VOCABULARY Wealth and poverty

a Match 1–6 with a–f to make sentences.

1 [b] The charity helps people who are
2 [ ] I've been lucky. I've never experienced any
3 [ ] We had to sell our car to
4 [ ] You'll get into debt if you don't learn to
5 [ ] The boom was a time of economic
6 [ ] They've got three cars, so they're obviously

a make ends meet.
b destitute.
c live within your means.
d well off.
e hardship.
f prosperity.

b <u>Underline</u> the correct words to complete the conversation.

A How would you describe your early life?
B Well, life was pretty tough. There was a lot of financial ¹<u>hardship</u> / risk.
A Where were you brought up?
B In a rather ²sparse / deprived area with poor housing and not many amenities.
A Were you very poor?
B No, not really. We weren't exactly ³poverty / impoverished. We were never rich but never ⁴destitute / well off either. We had just enough money to live on and were careful to live ⁵affluent / within our means.
A Now that you've become rich and have a large ⁶available / disposable income, how has your life changed?
B Well, obviously I don't have to worry about ⁷wealth / making ends meet. We live in a nice house in an affluent area.
A And are you happier?
B A good question. I would say my life is pretty comfortable now, but ⁸prosperity / poverty doesn't always necessarily bring you happiness.

c ▶ 03.01 Listen and check.

3 PRONUNCIATION Word stress

a ▶ 03.02 Listen to the words in the box. What stress pattern do they have? Complete the table with the words.

~~neighbouring~~ charity poverty destitute
relatives enrolment everyone volunteer
requirement improvement nutritious

Ooo	oOo	ooO
neighbouring		

3B | I WAS EXPECTING IT TO BE TOUGH

1 GRAMMAR Future in the past; Narrative tenses

a Match 1–8 with a–h to make sentences.

1 [f] She was leaving for the station
2 [ ] Apparently she was going to tell me
3 [ ] I thought I would be waiting a while,
4 [ ] We were about to head to the airport
5 [ ] One day I would become a great salesperson,
6 [ ] I was supposed to study Italian
7 [ ] I was to have stayed in Bangkok for a year
8 [ ] I was about to accept a new job

a but ended up with a degree in sociology.
b but never had the right opportunity.
c but actually stayed for three.
d when my manager asked me into his office.
e when we heard about the pilots' strike.
f when her phone rang.
g even if I was never to have much confidence.
h so I bought myself a coffee.

b Read some sentences from a story about Oliver Broom, a man who travelled to Australia by bike to watch a cricket match. Underline the correct words to complete the sentences.

1 In late 2008, Oliver Broom _was working_ / worked in London.
2 Having graduated six years before, he was earn / earning a good salary.
3 It seemed he was having / had a bright future.
4 A good friend had been / was seriously injured on holiday some time before.
5 This had made him question what he has done / was doing with his life.
6 On top of that, he has / had just split up with his girlfriend.
7 He suddenly decided he would / might cycle to Australia.
8 He worked out a route which had to / would take him through over 20 countries.
9 The last leg was from Darwin to Brisbane, which was / is going to be another 5,000 kilometres.
10 He said he should / would spend the first few months in Europe.
11 No sooner had he arrived in Thailand than he was suddenly struck down with dengue fever and was hospitalised / hospitalising.
12 Oli cycled into Brisbane the very day the cricket match was to start / has started.

c ▶03.03 Listen to the whole story and check your answers.

2 VOCABULARY Landscape features

a Match adjectives 1–8 with nouns a–h to make collocations.

1 [c] arid   a coastline
2 [ ] empty   b waters
3 [ ] pristine   c desert
4 [ ] rocky   d beaches
5 [ ] rugged   e moorland
6 [ ] sheer   f cliffs
7 [ ] turquoise   g slopes
8 [ ] wooded   h ground

b Underline the correct words to complete the email.

Hello all,

This place is amazing. It's a tropical paradise with everything you could ask for: pristine beaches, ¹dull / _calm_ / cold turquoise waters to swim in and a forest canopy ²full / rich / good with wildlife. Yesterday we took a boat trip and could see the rugged ³beach / coastline / shore from the sea. It has dramatic, sheer cliffs, and we got a chance to see birds nesting on the cliff ⁴side / hanger / face.

Today we hiked inland through rich, green meadows and up the ⁵angled / wooded / slanting slopes of the valleys. The view from the top was stunning! To one side, we could see ⁶dense / heavy / high forest and to the other, dry, rocky ground with hardly any vegetation. Tomorrow we are planning to go to the north where the terrain is completely different, with open, ⁷empty / busy / wide moorland that stretches for miles. As you approach the sea, there are massive ⁸beach / sand / cove dunes, apparently. I can't wait.

Love to you all,

Tina

3 PRONUNCIATION Different pronunciations of t

a ▶03.04 Listen to the sentences and notice how t is pronounced in the examples. Complete the table with the phrases in the box.

biggest egg   can't find   What a   it's so   ~~got amazing~~
can't ask   great in   biggest fish   great cook   ~~got four~~

/t/ pronounced	/t/ not pronounced
got amazing	got four

3C EVERYDAY ENGLISH
To cut a long story short

1 USEFUL LANGUAGE
Paraphrasing and summarising

a Underline the correct words to complete the conversation.

ALEX Hi, Dario. So what's this news you wanted to tell me?

DARIO Well, it really is quite exciting. [1]*Generally* / *Basically*, I have decided not to start work just yet.

ALEX Not work? But I thought you had a job offer.

DARIO I have, but, you know, we've only just graduated and I've been studying, taking exams, revising and so on for years. [2]*Shortly* / *In a nutshell*, I fancy doing something different and going somewhere new.

ALEX [3]*In other words* / *Said differently*, you're going travelling again.

DARIO But not just for pleasure. I did some reading, talked to some people, did some desk research, sent off some emails and [4]*to cut a long story short* / *that is to say*, I'm off to Uganda.

ALEX Wow! Africa. To do what?

DARIO Well, I wanted to do something meaningful, you know, help others. Give something back.

ALEX Not like people like me then!

DARIO No, [5]*what I meant was* / *my meaning was* that for me it's important to test myself a bit. Get out of the comfort zone. So I'm going to help build a primary school.

ALEX A school? That will be amazing! You out in the African heat and me at my hot desk at the bank. That just about sums it up. So, when are you off?

DARIO In two weeks. Can't wait. So much to do.

ALEX Can I just say ... How shall I put this? I'm very proud.

b ▶03.05 Listen and check.

c Complete the sentences with the phrases in the box. There may be more than one possible answer.

~~in a nutshell~~   to put it another way   in other words
that is to say   to cut a long story short   what I meant was

1 My job is quite difficult to explain but, _in a nutshell_, I help companies find solutions.
2 How did I end up here in China? Well, _____, I got a teaching job here 20 years ago.
3 Sorry, but that's not my point – _____ that the young should support older people.
4 People waste so much money on clothes, fast food, music … _____, stuff they don't need.
5 **A** Hmm, it could be at five o'clock ... or maybe six.
  B _____, you don't know!
6 People who eat their five a day, _____ fruit and vegetables, probably stay fitter.

2 PRONUNCIATION
Consonant clusters across two words

a Match the underlined letters 1–8 with the consonant clusters a–h.

1 [h] just gra̲duated   a /mw/
2 [ ] difficult to e̲x̲plain   b /ŋʃ/
3 [ ] de̲sk r̲esearch   c /stf/
4 [ ] so̲mew̲here new   d /zpr/
5 [ ] somethi̲n̲g m̲eaningful   e /kspl/
6 [ ] the you̲n̲g s̲hould support f /ŋm/
7 [ ] not ju̲st f̲or pleasure   g /skr/
8 [ ] vegetable̲s p̲robably   h /stgr/

b ▶03.06 Listen and check.

3D SKILLS FOR WRITING
The view is stunning

1 READING

a Read the review. Are the sentences true or false, or is there not enough information to be sure?

1 Geographically, Istanbul is perfectly situated.
2 The ferries run 24 hours a day.
3 Locals seem to enjoy eating and drinking.
4 You are not really aware of history in a city like this.
5 There are no skyscrapers in the city.
6 Some of the palaces have beautiful interiors.

b Read the review again. Complete the sentences with the words in the box.

> ~~vastness~~   by boat   negotiate
> buildings   cruise   traffic jams

1 Visitors are initially stunned by the __vastness__ of Istanbul.
2 The writer loves cities where you can commute _____.
3 A _____ along the Bosphorus gives you a historical view of the city.
4 There are regular _____ on the city's streets.
5 The city has an amazing mix of _____, from fortresses to mosques.
6 One place you must visit is a bazaar, where you can try to _____.

2 WRITING SKILLS Descriptive language; Writing briefly

a Complete the text with the words in the box.

> breathtaking   heart-stopping   freshly baked
> highly recommended   absolutely delicious
> ~~long weekend~~   stunning views   excellent value for money

Alan B
FROM DARWIN

We chose the Doubletree Hilton for our recent [1]long weekend in Istanbul and we were not disappointed. On arrival, we were presented with [2]_____ cookies and then shown to our room with [3]_____ of the sea and the Princes' Islands in the distance. We were on the Asian side, which meant there were slightly fewer tourists, but within a stone's throw of the hotel, streets lined with restaurants were all serving [4]_____ dishes. We could access all the tourist attractions on a [5]_____ taxi ride through busy traffic and enormous crowds, where people are buzzing past you at every moment. One other means of reaching the sights is the ferries – they're always packed but are [6]_____. Some of the sights were [7]_____ and the mix of up-to-the-minute and back-in-time makes Istanbul a must-see city. It's [8]_____.

Like · Comment · Share   👍 56   💬 7

TRAVEL
CITY BREAK OF THE WEEK ...

ISTANBUL

With one foot in Europe and the other in Asia, Istanbul is undoubtedly one of the greatest and largest cosmopolitan cities in the world. Whether you arrive from the airport on the east or the west, you will be stunned by the sheer size of the city. Its perfect geographic position has made it a target for emperors throughout history, and nothing takes you back in time more than a cruise along the Bosphorus, the river that not only divides the city but also acts as its lifeblood, ferrying thousands of commuters back and forth all day long. There is nothing to beat a city where you can go to work by ferry and relax on the water for half an hour at the beginning of your day.

Throughout the city, the traffic is loud and frequently gridlocked: taxis and buses fight for space and angry motorists use their horns liberally. Yet wherever you go, people are continually taking time out from the bustle of the city to sip tea or coffee, grab some cake or a kebab, or simply stop to chat.

The tourist sees history all around, from the wooded slopes leading down to the waterfront to the imposing fortresses atop the hills. The most ornate and intricate mosques of great architectural splendour are set amid the rapidly growing new commercial buildings soaring to the sky.

The smells and sounds of the city will be a lasting memory, as will the picturesque waterfront walks and the sumptuous décor of some of the palaces. Haggle in the bazaars, smell the fragrance of the spices, be amazed by the sheer size of the city. Have no doubt, Istanbul will delight you.

3 WRITING

a Write a review (200 words) of a recent trip you have taken to post on a travel website. Remember to use descriptive phrases to describe the place and your accommodation. Use these notes to help you:

- Introduce the destination. History? Size? Sights? Access?
- Describe your accommodation. Type? Price? Facilities?
- What was good and what was bad?

UNIT 3
Reading and listening extension

1 READING

a Read the blog. Put the words in the correct order to make sentences about it.

1 work because / adventurous / the author / he is / loves his

_____

2 from working / doing expedition / very different / in a hospital / medicine is

_____

3 on an expedition / would benefit / the author thinks / from working / that all doctors

_____

b Read the blog again. Tick (✓) the correct answer.

1 The author feels that he has … .
   a ☐ been able to choose his career
   b ✓ been lucky with his job
   c ☐ been self-indulgent in his work

2 He has worked in … .
   a ☐ a wide variety of landscapes
   b ☐ mountainous regions
   c ☐ the places he likes most

3 For an expedition doctor, medical skills are … .
   a ☐ as important as practical skills
   b ☐ more important than practical skills
   c ☐ less important than practical skills

4 Expedition doctors sometimes have to use unusual techniques because … .
   a ☐ they keep their equipment in a rucksack
   b ☐ unexpected things can happen
   c ☐ they don't have the resources of a hospital

5 On his first training course, the author … .
   a ☐ learned about caring for people's teeth
   b ☐ had to pull out someone's tooth
   c ☐ decided he didn't want to be a dentist

6 The author works for ethical companies because … .
   a ☐ he wants to make sure that his clients are safe at all times during the expedition
   b ☐ he feels uncomfortable about the difference between rich tourists and poor local people
   c ☐ they organise expeditions in the remote areas he enjoys visiting

c Imagine you are doing your job, or a job you would like to have, in a different country or in difficult conditions. Write a blog post about it. Include the answers to these questions:

- Where are you working?
- Who are you working with?
- What is the landscape like?
- What are the challenges?
- What do you enjoy or dislike about the job?

TRUST ME – I'm an expedition doctor

Ever since I was a young child, I've had a taste for adventure, but I never imagined I'd be able to indulge this passion at regular intervals because of my chosen career.

My work as an expedition doctor has taken me all over the world, from mosquito-infested swamps in Botswana to the untouched wilderness of Antarctica. However, my favourite trips, and the ones in which I now specialise, are those involving mountains. Never do I feel more inspired by nature than when I look up at their towering peaks and begin to prepare myself mentally for the challenges ahead.

I trained as a doctor in the UK, but there was little in that training to prepare me for strapping up a broken leg during a storm on the almost sheer side of a mountain! In fact, I'd say that medical skills are towards the bottom of the list of job requirements after stamina, flexibility, problem-solving and communication.

This kind of medicine is a million miles away from the controlled, sterile environment of a hospital, and your medical kit basically consists of whatever you can carry, so you sometimes have to be prepared to improvise. For example, I've learned that some drugs can be used for several conditions, and I've even had to resort to cutting branches off a small tree to make a splint to support a broken arm.

That isn't to say that you can't train to be an expedition doctor; on the contrary, there are some excellent courses available. Not only do they teach medical techniques, but also practical skills such as carrying out risk assessments, crossing rivers safely and using satellite phones. The first course I took included a module on expedition dentistry, though I must admit I still don't like the idea of pulling out someone's tooth!

I do most of my work for adventure travel companies that organise trips to remote places. When I started out, these trips were pretty rare, but they have become much more mainstream now that we've all seen celebrities climbing Kilimanjaro or watched reality shows about people surviving in jungles.

I do have mixed feelings about all these people with large amounts of disposable income coming to impoverished areas just for their own enjoyment, so I try to make sure that the companies I work for have high ethical standards and benefit the local communities. And of course, tourism provides employment and it also opens the eyes of affluent visitors to the hardship that many people are forced to endure.

I realise that this kind of life isn't for everyone, but I'd recommend that all doctors try it at least once, if only to make them appreciate the comforts of their usual working environment!

2 LISTENING

a ▶ 03.07 Listen to Gemma and her mum talking about adventurous women. Tick (✓) the correct answer.

1 Which sentence best summarises Gemma's attitude?
a ☐ She thinks that life had more potential for excitement in the past.
b ☐ The women's stories make her want excitement in her own life.
c ☐ She is disappointed that her mum isn't more adventurous.

2 Which sentence best summarises her mum's attitude?
a ☐ She thinks that most of the world's challenges have already been achieved.
b ☐ She focuses on the negative aspects of adventure.
c ☐ She is worried that Gemma will put herself in danger.

b ▶ 03.07 Listen again. Match people 1–4 with jobs a–d.

1 ☐ Gertrude Bell   a astronaut
2 ☐ Amelia Earhart   b pilot
3 ☐ Martha Gellhorn   c journalist
4 ☐ Valentina Tereshkova   d government adviser

c Are the sentences true or false, or is there not enough information to be sure?

1 Gemma's mum has travelled in jungles and deserts.
2 Gemma is impressed by the fact that many explorers have become famous.
3 Gertrude Bell's role in shaping modern Iraq was extremely positive.
4 A lot of men had flown across the Atlantic before Amelia Earhart did it.
5 Gemma's mum thinks that activities like Amelia Earhart's are too dangerous.
6 She says that Gemma isn't rich enough to be an explorer.
7 Martha Gellhorn reported mainly on wars in America during the Great Depression.
8 Gemma thinks that environmental problems will force us into more space exploration.

d Write a conversation between two people who are discussing the challenges of going to the moon. Think about these questions or use ideas of your own:

- Would the people be interested in taking part in an expedition to the moon? Why? / Why not?
- What do they think would be the main challenges?
- How would they feel if someone in their family went to the moon?

 **Review and extension**

1 GRAMMAR AND VOCABULARY

Correct the errors in the underlined words.

1 The journey not only will be longer but more expensive.
  Not only will the journey be longer but more expensive.
2 The staff not only were helpful but very patient.
3 He knew that nobody was to notice he was missing for at least two hours.
4 Under no circumstances confidential documents should be removed from the building.
5 The teachers were never available when we had needed them.
6 The atmosphere was really strange, as if something awful would happen.
7 Never before we have received complaints.
8 I would like a trial period. Only then I will be sure if I like the service.
9 I became very upset when the bus had broken down and the trip was cancelled.
10 As the number of homes increased, the amount of wildarness decreased.
11 Fields cover the lower valley and extend into wooded pools.
12 The film shows the beauty of the rain-forest set to music.

2 WORDPOWER Idioms: Landscapes

Rewrite the sentences. Replace the underlined words with the words in the box. Make any changes needed.

get bogged down   be swamped   ~~a drop in the ocean~~
an uphill struggle   be out of the woods

1 I'm trying to save money to buy a car, but the amount I have so far is nowhere near enough.
  I'm trying to save money to buy a car, but the amount I have so far is a drop in the ocean.
2 I found maths really difficult at school. I tried really hard, but I never seemed to make any progress.
3 My cat has been really ill, but the vet has told us that her life is no longer in danger. The kids will be happy!
4 My husband is really stressed – he has so much work on at the moment.
5 My sister's really good at looking at a problem and seeing a solution – I just get too involved in the details.

⟳ REVIEW YOUR PROGRESS

Look again at Review your progress on p. 42 of the Student's Book. How well can you do these things now?
3 = very well   2 = well   1 = not so well

I CAN ...	
emphasise positive and negative experiences	☐
describe journeys and landscapes	☐
paraphrase and summarise	☐
write a travel review.	☐

4A THAT LITTLE VOICE IN YOUR HEAD

1 GRAMMAR Noun phrases

a Put the words in the correct order to complete the introduction to a podcast.

1 Gloria Green, / best-selling author / guides, / the / healthy living / of / is today's guest .
Gloria Green, the best-selling author of healthy living guides, is today's guest.

2 published / recently / her / book, *Staying Alive*, is a complete A–Z of health and fitness .

_____

_____

3 getting / of / people / ages / all / to eat and drink sensibly has become / life's / work / her .

_____

_____

4 story / life / her / rags-to-riches / is living proof that dreams can come true .

_____

_____

5 easy-to-follow / her / apps / keep-fit / top sales charts all over the world .

_____

_____

b Improve the underlined sections by rewriting them as a single noun phrase. Use the patterns in the box.

1 I went to see a film. It was great. It was science fiction.
a great science-fiction film
2 And he's won the match with that shot which he judged perfectly!
3 Perhaps one day they'll be able to solve the problem that the climate is changing.
4 Have you ever tried cooking anything Thai – something like a green curry?
5 These paintings are the life's work of my uncle.
6 I won't get bored this weekend – I've got to do plenty of things.

Noun patterns

1 article + adjective + compound noun + noun
2 determiner + adverb + adjective + noun
3 article + compound noun + noun
4 pronoun + preposition + article + adjective + adjective + noun
5 possessive + noun + 's + noun + 's + noun
6 noun + *to* + infinitive

2 VOCABULARY Instinct and reason

a Complete the conversation with the words in the box.

subconsciously   on impulse   rational   spontaneous
gut instinct   think it over   ~~weigh up~~   think twice

A How do you decide to buy something?
B Well, it depends on what it is.
A What do you mean?
B If it's a house, for instance, I'd [1] _weigh up_ the advantages and disadvantages first and then [2]_____ for a while.
A So you tend to think logically?
B Yes, I suppose I'm a [3]_____ thinker. How about you?
A Well, I'd probably go with my [4]_____ in that situation.
B So you'd buy a house [5]_____, without thinking?
A Not necessarily, but I'd know [6]_____ that it was the right thing to do. Don't you ever make a [7]_____ decision?
B Yes, of course. I wouldn't [8]_____ about buying a new pair of shoes! I love to keep up with fashion!

b ▶ 04.01 Listen and check.

c Underline the correct words to complete the sentences.

1 She is always very *personable* / *reasonable* / *capable* and fair in her judgement.
2 A lot of students are *self-conscious* / *self-employed* / *selfish* when they make mistakes.
3 Japanese employees are renowned for being *conscious* / *conscientious* / *content*.
4 A lot of people are very *sensitive* / *senseless* / *sensible* and don't like criticism.
5 Some people are totally *emotional* / *rational* / *subjective* and don't allow feelings to interfere.
6 Actors appear to be *self-controlled,* / *self-confident,* / *selfless,* but in fact they are often shy.
7 I am very generous, whereas my brother is very *unconscious* / *self-conscious* / *money-conscious*.
8 The *senseless* / *sensitive* / *sensible* approach is to take our time and think it through.

4B HE GOT HIMSELF LOCKED IN A SHED

1 GRAMMAR Structures with *have* and *get*

a Complete the story. Match 1–8 with a–h to make sentences.

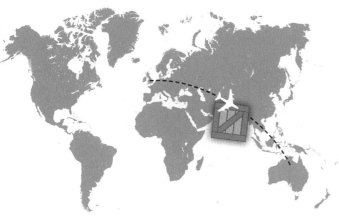

1 [h] In the 1950s, an Australian got
2 ☐ While saving up for a return flight home to Australia, he had
3 ☐ Finding himself with no money, he got a friend
4 ☐ He had it specially
5 ☐ They had the crate
6 ☐ In India, customs officials had
7 ☐ On arrival, he had hoped
8 ☐ He got

a designed so he could sit or lie down in it during the trip.
b labelled as paint for a fictitious shoe company in Australia.
c the crate unloaded, and it was then left upside down in the sun.
d his wallet stolen and had no money for a ticket.
e driven from the airport to the city centre and got home in time for his daughter's birthday.
f to have the invoice paid cash on delivery, but the crate was left in a shed and he escaped.
g to build a packing crate large enough for him to sit in.
h himself flown back home from London not as a passenger, but as a package.

b Underline the correct words to complete the sentences.

1 My hair is getting very long. I will have to *get it cut* / *get it to cut* soon.
2 When I was living abroad as a student, I used to get my parents *send* / *to send* me my favourite snacks from home.
3 Our house was getting too small for the family, so we *had it extended* / *got it to extend*.
4 She is starting up a new business and is getting her friends *to help* / *helped* her.
5 That suit fits so perfectly you must have *had made it* / *had it made* for you.
6 The offices needed renovating, so we had an architect *draw* / *drawing* up some plans.
7 When we moved, we got *to forward our post* / *our post forwarded* to our new address.
8 I had had the room *to set up* / *set up* in advance, so we were ready to start on time.

2 VOCABULARY Memory

a Complete the conversation with the words in the box. There may be more than one possible answer.

> painful memory ~~cast~~ a vivid memory come to mind
> a lasting memory slipped triggers treasure

A If you [1] ___cast___ your mind back to your early life as a child, what do you remember?
B I find the smell of cut grass always [2]_____ a memory of my childhood.
A Do you have [3]_____ of that time?
B Well, to be honest, many things are just a distant memory now. Although I suppose one thing I do [4]_____ is the memory of family holidays by the sea.
A Do you have any recollection at all of your school days?
B Well, I have [5]_____ of the day I started school. One boy wouldn't stop crying. I still remember some of my teachers as well, but other things have completely [6]_____ my mind.
A Do any of your school friends [7]_____?
B I do have a rather [8]_____ of a friend who moved away suddenly one day and I never saw again.

b Underline the correct words to complete the story.

When I was very young, I [1]*say* / *remind* / *remember* we always went to Italy on holiday. In those days, it was quite unusual to go abroad, but I have a vivid [2]*memory* / *souvenir* / *photo* of our suitcases being loaded onto the train before our two-day journey to Lake Como. Another image that [3]*comes* / *goes* / *flashes* to mind is seeing the green-shuttered hotel for the first time as we arrived at our destination after what seemed like an incredibly long journey. We used to collect sugar wrappers and coasters as [4]*items* / *souvenirs* / *memories* and I will never forget buying a small wooden sailing boat to take home. In the evenings, we would walk by the lake, and I have a [5]*vague* / *dull* / *thick* memory of paddling in it at sunset. I also [6]*recall* / *remind* / *think* another time when my brothers put me in a rowing boat and pretended to push me out into the middle of the lake. I will never [7]*forget* / *forgo* / *forgive* the sheer terror as they waved me off! I am getting old now, but I still have my photo album to [8]*refresh* / *run* / *tip* my memory. It was a very special time in my life, and I will always [9]*see* / *treasure* / *mind* the memories.

3 PRONUNCIATION Sentence stress

a ▶04.02 Listen and underline the stressed syllables in the sentences.

1 I remember when I was very young.
2 We always went on holiday to Italy.
3 In the evening, we would walk by the lake.
4 My brothers put me in a rowing boat.
5 I still have my photo album to refresh my memory.

4C EVERYDAY ENGLISH
I see where you're coming from

1 USEFUL LANGUAGE
Being tactful in formal discussions

a Complete the conversation with the phrases in the box.

> ~~What did you think~~
> I see where you're coming from
> No offence intended
> In fact, if you don't mind me saying so
> OK, I take your point
> I beg to differ
> With all due respect

A ¹ _What did you think_ of the presentation?

B ² _____, but I found it dull.

A I think ³ _____, but ⁴ _____.

B So you found it interesting?

A Well, not exactly interesting, but dull is a little harsh.

B ⁵ _____, it's much better to be frank. It was boring.

A ⁶ _____. It wasn't that interesting, but we need to be more supportive.

B I disagree. ⁷ _____, he needs to be told.

A I'll leave that to you then. You're his manager!

b ▶ 04.03 Listen and check.

c Put the words in the correct order to make the responses. Add any punctuation needed.

1 **A** They really make us work hard here, don't they?
   B it / about / me / tell .
   Tell me about it.

2 **A** The customers are quite demanding as well.
   B telling / you're / me .
   _____

3 **A** It would be good to make a few changes, wouldn't it?
   B due / respect / only just / all / with / started / you've .
   _____

4 **A** The problem is we really don't have enough people in the team.
   B take / I / very new / you're / your / still / but / point.
   _____

5 **A** Do you think we should tell the management?
   B me saying / it's probably / don't mind / best to wait / so / if you .
   _____

6 **A** You think I should wait a while?
   B head / on / nail / the / hit / you've / the .
   _____

2 PRONUNCIATION
Homophones in words and connected speech

a ▶ 04.04 Listen and match the homophones in the box to the underlined words in the sentences.

> ~~ate~~ sail hear died break aloud weak blue

1 I have eight brothers. _____ate_____
2 When I was a child, I was only allowed to eat sweets once a week. _____
3 My mother dyed the sheets blue. _____
4 I had to brake very late to avoid an accident. _____
5 I eat out at least three times a week. _____
6 They want to place the new conference table here. _____
7 The strong winds blew the parasols over. _____
8 This coat was half price in the sale. _____

1 READING

a Read the newspaper article. Are the sentences true or false?

1 Italy play in dark blue shirts.
2 Scottish rugby fans were disappointed that Tommy didn't choose to play for their team.
3 He played youth international rugby for Scotland.
4 He decided he wanted to play for Italy after changing schools.
5 When he played against Scotland, some players from the Scottish team made jokes.
6 He started playing rugby seriously in his teens.
7 Both his parents played international rugby.
8 He still plays rugby in southwest France.

b Read the article again. Put the events in the order they happened.

- [ ] He moved to France to play rugby for Perpignan.
- [1] His uncle played for Scotland.
- [ ] He went to South Africa to attend school and play more rugby.
- [ ] He started speaking English when the family moved to England.
- [ ] He played his first full game for Italy.
- [ ] He was born in Vicenza, Italy.
- [ ] He played for Italy against Scotland.

2 WRITING SKILLS Organising information; Showing time relationships

a Read the article again. Look at the pairs of sentences. What is the interval between events? Tick (✓) the correct box.

	Immediate	Short interval	Long interval
1 Being born. Starting to speak English.			✓
2 Speaking to the coach. Deciding to play for Italy.			
3 Deciding to play for Italy. Being selected by Italy.			
4 Changing schools. Realising he wanted to play professional rugby.			
5 Playing sports. Playing rugby.			
6 Choosing to play for Italy. Playing against Scotland.			

A Choice of Blue

Tommaso Allan, Tommy to his friends, is a rugby union player who made his full international debut in the light blue shirt of Italy in November 2013 against Australia. Since then, he has been a regular member of the team, much to the disappointment of Scottish fans who had hoped he would wear the dark blue of Scotland.

When we met in a café in Perpignan in southwest France, where he was playing professional rugby at the time, he explained how things happened. 'I had played for Scotland at most of the youth ages, under-nineteens and under-twenties, and so on, but when I moved to France in the summer of 2013, I still wasn't sure which international team I would play for.' It was only when the Italian coach asked him if he wanted to play for Italy that he made up his mind and chose Italy. Shortly afterwards, he was selected to play in the game against Australia. Soon after that, he was playing for Italy *against* Scotland and thoroughly enjoying it, despite a certain amount of teasing from players he knew on the Scottish team.

Tommy was born in Vicenza, Italy, in 1993 to an Italian mother and a Scottish father. Until he was eight, he lived in Italy and Italian was his first language. It was only when he moved to England in 2001 that he started speaking English. As a kid, he played football and basketball and didn't particularly like rugby, despite it being in his blood. 'My uncle played for Scotland in 1990 and 1991 and then for South Africa, and my dad was a good player, too,' he pointed out, adding that his mother also played for the Italian women's team! It wasn't until his teens that he started playing rugby seriously, playing for a club at weekends and flying to South Africa during school holidays to attend a rugby-playing school there. 'I learned such a lot from my time in South Africa, and I still go back regularly,' he told me. Having changed schools in England to play more rugby, he soon realised he wanted to make a living from the game.

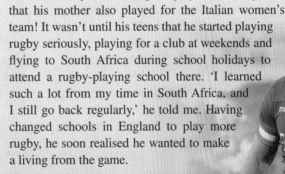

So how did he enjoy life in France? 'It's a beautiful country to live in,' I remember him saying as he sipped a glass of sparkling water.

He may have loved France, but a few short years after our conversation, Tommy would return to Italy to play for Benetton Rugby. More recently, in 2021, he moved back to England, joining Premiership team Harlequins.

3 WRITING

a Write an article (250 words) about an interview with someone famous. Use direct quotes, time expressions and reported answers. Remember to include:

- the setting of the interview
- what they do
- how they discovered their interest or ability
- their recent experiences and future plans.

HOW TO MAKE GOOD DECISIONS

1 READING

a Read the article about decision-making. Complete this summary of the article with the words in the box.

> poor   mental   rational   useful   better

In order to make ¹_____ decisions, you need plenty of ²_____ energy. People with a lot of problems often make ³_____ decisions. There are several ⁴_____ strategies that can help us make decisions, but sometimes it is ⁵_____ simply to do what our instincts tell us.

b Read the article again. Match paragraphs 1–7 with summaries a–g.

a ☐ It says why the time of day affects our decision-making.
b ☐ It stresses the importance of our beliefs and opinions.
c ☐1 It asks why people are bad at making decisions,
d ☐ It gives an idea for uncovering our inner thoughts.
e ☐ It explains why people with difficult lives may make bad decisions.
f ☐ It talks about how we use facts in our decision-making.
g ☐ It gives advice about how to make a decision less personal.

c Read the text again. Tick (✓) the correct answer.

1 Why is it surprising that people make bad decisions?
  a ☐ Everyone has time to make good decisions.
  b ☑ We should be able to understand the factors involved and see which are important.
  c ☐ We should learn from other people's decisions.

2 Why do people with difficult lives suffer more 'decision fatigue' than other people?
  a ☐ They aren't educated enough about health and finance.
  b ☐ They have to make more decisions than others.
  c ☐ They use a lot of mental energy for everyday life.

3 Why is it a good idea to pretend a friend is making the decision?
  a ☐ It helps you to step back from the problem.
  b ☐ You will want to give your friend good advice.
  c ☐ Your friends usually make good decisions and you want to be like them.

4 Why do people often want as much information as they can get?
  a ☐ It helps them list advantages and disadvantages.
  b ☐ More information always means a better decision.
  c ☐ It is part of human nature to want facts.

5 How can flipping a coin help you?
  a ☐ It makes a choice for you so you don't have to.
  b ☐ It makes you realise that you do have a preference.
  c ☐ It shows that a random decision can be a good one.

6 Why should we consider how we'll feel about a decision in later life?
  a ☐ We'll make sensible decisions about spending money.
  b ☐ We'll avoid being sorry about the way we have lived.
  c ☐ We'll be wiser when we are older.

1 We all like to think that we are rational thinkers, but poor decisions and choices are evident all around us: staying in bad relationships or boring jobs, starting smoking, eating too much junk food, taking out loans we know we can't repay; the list goes on. So why can't we make better decisions? Surely we know how to weigh the advantages and disadvantages in a situation and come to a sensible conclusion? One reason appears to be what psychologists call 'decision fatigue': the idea that we all have a limited supply of energy for making decisions and exerting self-control.

2 Studies are increasingly finding evidence that our life circumstances play a huge part in our ability to be rational. If you are ground down by everyday struggles, you have less mental energy for good decisions. These findings go a long way to explaining why people with problems such as poverty or poor housing so often appear to make irrational decisions – for example, in relation to their health or financial affairs.

3 However, this research does point to the fact that deciding things early in the day is likely to lead to better outcomes. Most of us will have had the experience of going to bed with a seemingly unsolvable problem, only to wake up with a flash of inspiration the next morning. So decisions made when we feel least tired are more likely to be the right ones.

4 Another worthwhile strategy is to pretend that you are advising a friend (who can be imaginary!) rather than relating decisions to your own life. This creates a distance between you and the issues in question, and can help you to think logically rather than emotionally.

5 People often advise making lists of pros and cons and then prioritising the items in each list. This can certainly be helpful, but we need to be careful not to overthink every decision. The human mind is programmed to hate uncertainty, so many of us feel compelled to gather as much information as we possibly can before making a decision. However, we can overestimate the value of information, and sometimes it is better simply to go with our gut instinct.

6 Try this simple experiment: take a coin and assign a decision to each side. Then flip the coin and, before it lands, ask yourself which way you are *hoping* it will come down. This way you may find that you knew the answer subconsciously all along.

7 Perhaps the most important thing we can do to minimise the possibility of regret is to make sure that our decisions are in line with our life values; in other words, have a life vision and be true to it. Instead of asking ourselves questions such as 'Which option is safer?' or 'Which option is best financially?,' it is much better to ask 'How will I feel about this when I'm 70?'

d Write a short article for a popular magazine about how to make decisions. Remember to include:

- examples of common decisions that people have to make
- a list of top tips
- the reason for each tip.

2 LISTENING

a ▶ 04.05 Listen to the conversation between Leila and Hannah. Complete the sentences.

1 Leila felt _embarrassed_ when she cried in the museum.
2 Leila's grandmother died when she was _____.
3 When she went to visit, her grandmother used to have a _____ delivered.
4 Leila and Hannah watched a documentary about people with _____ problems.
5 The documentary was about using _____ to trigger memories.
6 Implicit and explicit memories are stored in different parts of the _____.
7 When Hannah was younger, she travelled in _____.
8 Leila thought of a song she associates with her _____.

b ▶ 04.05 Listen again. Tick (✓) the correct box.

	Yes	No
1 Does Leila have a clear memory of her grandmother's living room?		✓
2 Does she remember what her grandmother's house smelled like?		
3 Has Hannah had similar experiences of something triggering a memory?		
4 Do explicit memories take conscious effort?		
5 Is the part of the brain that stores explicit memories stronger than the part that stores implicit memories?		
6 Does music have to be high quality to trigger profound emotions?		
7 Does Hannah find that classical music triggers memories for her as much as pop music?		
8 Can pieces of music remind you of particular people?		

c Write a conversation between two people discussing things that trigger memories for them. Use these questions to help you:

• Are the experiences triggered by music? By other sounds? By smell, taste or visual means?
• Are strong emotions triggered by one of these things?
• Why do you think they have this effect?

 # Review and extension

1 GRAMMAR AND VOCABULARY

Correct the errors in the underlined words.

1 Starting work with <u>the new company</u> can be pretty nerve-racking.
Starting work with a new company can be pretty nerve-racking.
2 <u>The first day of the group</u> in London was hard to forget; we were outsiders in a strange city.
3 The sudden increase in <u>personal computers' numbers</u> made the planet more connected.
4 We can't pay anyone else, but I'll help you <u>have the job done on time</u>.
5 Better care means <u>the old people</u> are living longer these days.
6 He is a very <u>racional</u> person – he always thinks things through very logically and unemotionally.
7 She is extremely <u>sensible</u> to what people say and often takes things much too personally.
8 The sales manager is very <u>self confident</u>. In fact, he sometimes comes across as arrogant.
9 When we got lost, we didn't panic – in fact, we were very <u>sensitive</u> and just retraced our steps.
10 They are very <u>conscient</u> of what they eat. They won't eat any processed foods.

2 WORDPOWER *mind*

Rewrite the sentences. Replace the underlined words with the words in the box. Make any changes needed.

put one's mind to it   cross one's mind
bear something in mind   read someone's mind
speak one's mind

1 I'm starting a coding class. I don't know anything about it but if I <u>try really hard</u>, I'll work it out.
I'm starting a coding class. I don't know anything about it but if I put my mind to it, I'll work it out.
2 Thanks for letting me know that you enjoy role play – <u>that's useful to know for</u> the next lesson.
3 If you don't agree with an action, you must <u>give your opinion</u>; otherwise, things will never change.
4 I can't believe how angry my friend is with me. She hates dancing, so <u>I didn't even think of inviting</u> her to my party!
5 You should have told me you wanted me to buy chocolate – I <u>don't know what you're thinking</u>.

🔄 REVIEW YOUR PROGRESS

Look again at Review your progress on p. 54 of the Student's Book. How well can you do these things now?
3 = very well   2 = well   1 = not so well

I CAN ...	
talk about using instinct and reason	☐
talk about memories and remembering	☐
use tact in formal discussions	☐
write a profile article.	☐

A PLACE WHERE YOU HAVE TO LOOK OVER YOUR SHOULDER

1 GRAMMAR Relative clauses

a Complete the sentences with the words in the box.

why ~~most of which~~ who which all of whom
where the result of which whose

1 A pickpocket recently admitted around a hundred offences, _most of which_ had been committed against tourists over the last six months.
2 A Turkish tourist _____ wallet had been stolen agreed to meet the thief.
3 A journalist interviewed other tourists on the street _____ the incident had taken place.
4 He talked to three tourists, _____ were carrying valuables in their rucksacks.
5 One tourist, _____ preferred not to give his name, had a wallet in his back pocket.
6 There are obvious reasons _____ tourists are such an easy target.
7 A lot of tourists carry cash, _____ is not very sensible.
8 There was an advertising campaign last year, _____ was a drop in pickpocketing crime.

b Match 1–8 with a–h to make sentences.

1 [f] We recruited a lot of staff last year,
2 [ ] I don't want to say anything
3 [ ] The menu has a limited number of dishes,
4 [ ] Whoever is last to leave
5 [ ] Spring is a time of year
6 [ ] The club takes on a lot of young players,
7 [ ] She was late to work on her first day,
8 [ ] I've met a lot of people while travelling,

a a few of whom are now close friends.
b should switch off the lights.
c a percentage of whom turn professional.
d I always look forward to.
e which was a bad sign.
f some of whom have done really well.
g most of which I've tried.
h that could be misunderstood.

2 VOCABULARY Crime and justice

a Complete the text with the words in the box.

assault community convicted goods life
~~possession~~ psychiatric sentences served solitary

Our reactions to crime are very personal and depend on our social situation and upbringing, according to a recent report from Swedish psychologists. Most people consider nonviolent crimes, such as [1] _possession_ of stolen [2]_____, to be minor compared to crimes that involve injury to people, such as violent [3]_____. Views on punishment are also changing, with the majority now seeing [4]_____ service as the most beneficial punishment for both the offender and the victims. It is increasingly felt that punishments like being held in [5]_____ confinement or being sentenced to [6]_____ imprisonment are less appropriate, and that [7]_____ help is necessary to rehabilitate criminals. It is also argued that those [8]_____ of certain crimes should have them removed from their records when the [9]_____ have been [10]_____ or shortly afterwards.

b Underline the correct words to complete the conversation.

A People commit all types of crime today. How do you think we should deal with these offenders?
B Well, it depends on the crime and the person who has been found [1]*wrong* / *guilty* of the crime.
A What about someone who has been [2]*punished* / *sentenced* to life imprisonment? Should they [3]*deliver* / *serve* the full sentence?
B In my opinion, a [4]*cut* / *reduced* sentence for good behaviour should be possible. Such offenders need to receive one-to-one [5]*counselling* / *punishment*.
A Do you think offenders need to be brought face-to-face with their [6]*crimes* / *victims*?
B Yes, I'd agree that in certain situations, a meeting could help both the victim and the offender.

3 PRONUNCIATION Sound and spelling: *s* and *ss*

a ▶ 05.01 Listen to the words in the box. How are the **bold** letters pronounced in each word? Complete the chart with the words.

compari~~s~~on mi**ss**ion occa**s**ion A**s**ian per**s**on Ru**ss**ian
pa**ss**ion impri**s**onment cou**s**in dismi**ss** pre**ss**ure colli**s**ion

/s/ (e.g., *lesson*)	/ʃ/ (e.g., *session*)	/ʒ/ (e.g., *measure*)	/z/ (e.g., *reason*)
comparison			

5B | IT'S ESSENTIAL TO HAVE THE RIGHT QUALIFICATIONS

1 GRAMMAR
Obligation, necessity and permission

a Complete the text using the words in the box.

> aren't really expected   English is mandatory
> has had to   was required   must do   is essential
> should be   is called on

Samya is a very unusual person. She became a pilot in her twenties with one of the world's fastest growing airlines. Globally, only 5% of pilots are female, so Samya [1] _has had to_ show great courage and determination to realise her dream of flying passengers all over the planet.

'Women [2] _____ to be in the cockpit,' she says, 'particularly in this part of the world.'

So how did she make it? For her 21st birthday present, she was given flying lessons and, within six months, she had been accepted onto a pilot training scheme. A lot of hard work [3] _____, but she made good progress and got a lot of support from her male classmates.

'A pilot [4] _____ to make a lot of quick decisions, and a calm manner [5] _____, particularly when flying in bad weather,' Samya goes on. 'Good communication skills are vital because you are constantly in communication with your copilot and air traffic control, for which good knowledge of [6] _____.' Many passengers are surprised to see that Samya is their pilot, and this adds a bit of pressure. 'As a woman, I feel I [7] _____ an even better job so that I make a good impression not just for the airline, but for my gender. I feel there [8] _____ more female pilots and that I am a role model for girls who might want to choose the same career.'

b Underline the correct words to complete the text.

I know a lot of people think my job working on a trawler is quite dangerous, but my employers [1]*are intended / are required / must* to do a thorough risk assessment to make sure it is as safe as possible. We are away for up to two weeks at a time because we are [2]*expected / known / wanted* to come back to port only when we have caught our target weight of fish. We [3]*are / have to / need* work 12 to 14 hours a day, and an ability to work even when seasick is [4]*definite / optional / mandatory*. Strength and good balance are [5]*fine / essential / useless,* and [6]*you can / you have / you must* to be able to work as part of a team. Sleeping facilities are limited, so a willingness to share bunks is [7]*good / needy / expected.* We live and work in close proximity to each other, so a good sense of humour is also a [8]*rule / use / requirement*.

2 VOCABULARY Employment

a Complete the crossword puzzle. Use the clues to name the employment sectors.

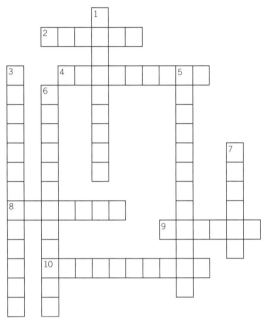

→ Across
2 oil, gas, solar, etc.
4 banking, accounting, investment, etc.
8 hotels, cruises, resorts, sightseeing, etc.
9 owned and managed by a government
10 industry and factories

↓ Down
1 cars, buses, trains, etc.
3 producing goods in large numbers
5 farming, crops, livestock
6 building houses, office blocks, bridges, etc.
7 selling to the general public

3 PRONUNCIATION Word stress: nouns and verbs

a ▶ 05.02 Listen. What is the stress pattern of the underlined words? Tick (✓) the correct box.

	Oo	oO
1 Could you give me your <u>contact</u> details?	✓	
2 We couldn't find any <u>record</u> of a meeting on that date.		
3 We <u>export</u> about 45% of our production.		
4 We are starting the <u>research</u> in Liberia next month.		
5 We need to <u>increase</u> the number of international contracts we get.		
6 We <u>produce</u> most of our own vegetables.		

5C EVERYDAY ENGLISH
I'd hazard a guess

1 USEFUL LANGUAGE
Recalling and speculating

a Complete the sentences with the words in the box.

> hazard   impression   memory
> presumably   ~~suppose~~   stands

1 **A** The beach is really rocky. There's no sand at all.
  B _Suppose_ you'd known, would you still have gone on holiday there?
2 **A** Who painted that picture?
  B I'm not sure. I'd _____ a guess at Monet.
3 **A** What time does the wedding ceremony start?
  B _____ it'll be some time in the morning.
4 **A** That holiday to Switzerland was amazing, wasn't it?
  B It was brilliant. What _____ out in my mind were the amazing views of the Alps.
5 **A** Who organised the golf trip last year?
  B If my _____ serves me correctly, it was Lisa Feng.
6 **A** The flight leaves on Thursday at 4 pm from Terminal 2.
  B Are you sure? I was under the _____ that all international flights leave from Terminal 1.

b Match the statements and questions 1–6 with the responses a–f.

1 [d] I thought I remembered you saying you played squash.
2 [ ] Have you ever been diving?
3 [ ] No doubt you've already researched the best restaurants in the neighbourhood.
4 [ ] Judging from your appearance, I'd hazard a guess at 30.
5 [ ] I was under the impression you spoke Thai.
6 [ ] Presumably you have a degree.

a No, I don't, although I worked in Pattaya for a couple of months.
b Well, actually, I went to university but I left after two years.
c Yes, I have. What stands out in my mind is seeing a huge turtle.
d That's right. Do you?
e Very good! I turn 31 next month.
f Of course! What else was I going to do while I was hungry on the train?

c ▶05.03 Listen and check.

d ▶05.04 Listen to the sentences and tick (✓) the correct box.

		Speculating	Recalling
1	I bet you it'll rain tomorrow just because it's the weekend.	✓	
2	I was under the impression it was open on Mondays.		
3	I'd hazard a guess you work in marketing of some sort.		
4	I'm guessing you're a sports fan.		
5	I'm sure I remember my father telling me that joke.		
6	No doubt you'll be surprised but I am actually Canadian.		
7	Suppose you'd been born in Germany, how different would your life be?		
8	What stands out for me about the eighties is the music.		
9	Without a shadow of a doubt, the value of gold will continue to rise.		

2 PRONUNCIATION Main stress

a ▶05.05 Listen and underline the word with the main stress in each phrase.

1 He's not just <u>any</u> footballer … he's the world's <u>best</u> footballer.
2 Some countries simply copy … while other countries create.
3 It's not just the money … it's the time and the money.
4 I don't know any jokes … I don't know any good jokes anyway.
5 The lesson wasn't just difficult … it was difficult and boring.

SKILLS FOR WRITING
It's a way of making the application process more efficient

Job Hunting: It's Complicated!

1 The job application process is a lot more complicated than it used to be and applicants need to be ready to show a wide range of skills simply to complete it. What's more, this process might be producing good applicants rather than people who will be able to do a good job.

2 In the past, a letter, an application form and a CV were usually enough. You sent them off, together with a reference that might or might not be followed up on. Today's applicants, on the other hand, have to be much better prepared. As well as assessing job opportunities, they need to keep their profile updated on a suitable networking website. It's helpful to include a good photo, probably different from the one on Facebook. In addition to updating the profile, they also need to ensure that it is regularly endorsed by people who have worked with them, ideally with a short comment.

3 Having seen a possible job, you need to apply through the correct route, often a website, and carry out all the steps promptly. Once the shortlist is ready, the next stage is often an automatically marked online questionnaire and, depending on those results, an application will move on or stop there. What's more, it is worth noting that up to this point there has been very little contact between humans in the whole process.

4 At the interview, there's an opportunity not only to express interest in the job, but also to respond to a wide range of questions designed to find out more about you. Besides the standard questions about achievements and aspirations, you may well be asked at least one simple but potentially quirky question that sets the final candidates apart from the rest. As well as answering questions, you may have to carry out a task. Certain companies have gone further and asked interviewees to read poetry or extracts from plays out loud in the hope that this brings out other aspects of the candidate's personality. Besides being of dubious value, this technique is probably pretty intimidating.

5 I agree that employers need to be absolutely sure about who they recruit since human resources are one of the major investments companies make. It is important, therefore, that the process is thorough. On the other hand, it is imperative that the system finds the best recruits, not necessarily just those who manage the process well.

1 READING

a Read the essay. Underline the correct words to complete the sentences.

1 Job applications have become more *expensive* / *time-consuming*.

2 References were *always* / *sometimes* followed up on.

3 It is important to keep your *online profile* / *application form* up to date.

4 Online questionnaires are usually *automatically* / *manually* assessed.

5 The interview often includes one *odd* / *factual* question.

6 Certain interviewers have been known to ask candidates to *complete an assignment* / *take a personality test*.

7 Reading poetry out loud is *valuable for employers* / *uncomfortable for interviewees*.

8 The tone of the concluding paragraph is *enthusiastic* / *cautious*.

b Read the essay again. Match paragraphs 1–5 with summaries a–e.

a ☐ Author's conclusion
b ☐ A description of the interview
c ☐ 1 Author states topic and introduces their point of view
d ☐ Comparison of past and present requirements
e ☐ A description of the first part of the recruitment process these days

2 WRITING SKILLS Essays;
Linking: addition and reinforcement

a Complete the sentences with the words in the box.

besides	as well as	~~furthermore, they~~
above	in addition	moreover

1 Online questionnaires are good for preselection. _Furthermore, they_ are cheap and easy to set up.

2 _____ to keeping your profile updated, you should get people to endorse you.

3 _____ details of your professional life, it is good to have a short description on your CV of other activities you do.

4 It is good to have a recent photo on your profile and, _____ all, to keep your contact details up to date.

5 Your CV should be attractive rather than dense. _____, too much detail can become tedious.

6 The job application process is long. _____, the competition is tough.

3 WRITING

a Write a short opinion essay (250 words) on the topic 'How does your online presence help you in the job market?' Offer ideas for finding and getting a job. Think about:

- your CV and online profile
- other social media
- personal activities
- some examples to support your ideas.

1 READING

a Read the article. Tick (✓) the best definition of 'restorative justice'.

1 ☐ a chance for the victim to have an influence on the kind of punishment a criminal is given

2 ☐ a meeting where the criminal says they're sorry to the victim

3 ☐ a meeting where the victim and the criminal discuss what happened and its consequences

4 ☐ a chance for the criminal to explain to the victim what led them to commit the crime

b Read the article again. Tick (✓) the advantages of restorative justice that are mentioned.

1 ✓ The criminal can say they're sorry.

2 ☐ It reduces prison costs for the state.

3 ☐ The victim gets a more realistic idea of the criminal's character.

4 ☐ The criminal better understands the effect of the crimes.

5 ☐ The criminal is less likely to commit another crime.

6 ☐ The victim and the criminal can support one another in the future.

7 ☐ It relieves pressure on the court system.

c Underline the correct words to complete the sentences.

1 Emily suffered *serious* / *minor* / *life-threatening* injuries in the attack.

2 She was *reluctant* / *eager* / *prepared* to take part in the restorative justice meeting.

3 When she met her attacker, she felt *angry* / *pleased* / *relieved*.

4 She could tell that he had had a *pleasant* / *badly behaved* / *difficult* life.

5 After the meeting, she felt *calmer* / *angrier* / *better informed* about what had happened.

6 Emily's attacker wants to change his *sentence* / *mind* / *behaviour*.

d Write a short essay about youth crime. Use these notes to help you:

- What do you think are the main reasons that young people commit crimes?
- What kind of punishments do you think are appropriate for young people?
- What do you think could be done to reduce levels of youth crime?

The day I looked my attacker in the eye

By Emily Brown

One day last summer, I was walking home late at night when a young man jumped out from behind some trees and grabbed my handbag. He knocked me to the ground and I suffered cuts to my face and arms. Thanks to security cameras in the area, the man was quickly arrested and convicted of robbery.

But despite being fit and relatively young, I couldn't put the incident out of my mind. I kept looking at my own son and asking myself how someone could do such a thing. My previous optimistic outlook turned to one of general suspicion; my self-confidence had vanished.

So when a woman from the youth service telephoned me and asked if I would be willing to take part in a restorative justice scheme, I jumped at the chance. She explained that it would involve a face-to-face meeting with the youth, who was still serving his prison sentence. I would have the chance to explain how his crime had affected me and to ask him any questions I wanted to.

I was incredibly nervous beforehand, but as soon as I saw my attacker sitting there, looking just as scared as me, I felt a weight lifted off my shoulders. I realised that I'd built him up in my mind into an evil and threatening character when really he was just a troubled young man who had so far had quite a hard life.

The idea of restorative justice is that it benefits both the victim and the perpetrator. For me, the crucial thing was to hear his apology. It also enabled me to put the incident in perspective and move on with my life. On his side, by meeting me, my attacker was obliged to acknowledge what he had done on a personal level, rather than seeing his crime as something abstract.

Evidence increasingly shows that this 'humanisation' of crime can have a strong preventive effect. While it is no substitute for prosecution in more serious cases, restorative justice is increasingly being used for young people who commit relatively minor crimes. This has the dual advantage of reducing future offences and preventing those young people from being burdened with a criminal record.

My friends said I was courageous to take part in the scheme, but actually I think it was courageous on the part of my attacker, too. He says he's serious about turning his life around and I hope that's true. I think it's essential that young people like him are given support and guidance, and I feel that restorative justice can help accomplish that goal.

2 LISTENING

a ▶ 05.06 Listen to the conversation. <u>Underline</u> the correct words to complete the sentences.

1 Speaker 1, Adriana, is *a soldier* / *a police officer* / *a lawyer*.
2 Speaker 2, Ben, is *a diver* / *an economist* / *an engineer*.
3 Speaker 3, Martina, is *a farmer* / *a store worker* / *a fruit picker*.

b ▶ 05.06 Listen again. Tick (✓) the correct box. Some questions have more than one answer.

	Adriana	Ben	Martina
1 Whose job is dangerous?	✓	✓	
2 Who says they enjoy the variety of their work?			
3 Who has to fill in a lot of forms?			
4 Who mentions earning a lot of money?			
5 Whose job is badly paid?			
6 Who works away from their family home?			
7 Who says their job is very physically tiring?			
8 Who dislikes their employer?			

c ▶ 05.06 Listen again. <u>Underline</u> the correct words to complete the sentences.

1 You *need* / *don't need* to be brave to be a police officer.
2 *Some* / *None* of Adriana's colleagues have been attacked.
3 It is *easy* / *not easy* for Adriana to combine her work and her home life.
4 Ben has worked for Engineers Without Borders for *more* / *less* than ten years.
5 He *still has to* / *doesn't have to* work if the working conditions are unsafe.
6 He *misses* / *doesn't miss* his family when he is away.
7 His job *is* / *isn't* very satisfying to him.
8 Martina *works* / *doesn't work* on the fruit farm all year.
9 Martina *thinks* / *doesn't think* that her wages are fair.
10 Martina *works* / *doesn't work* very long hours.

d Write a conversation between two people discussing the advantages and disadvantages of different jobs. Think about these questions or use ideas of your own:

- What would be your ideal job and why?
- What job would you least like to do and why?
- Which jobs have the highest and lowest salaries?
- Which jobs give the most satisfaction?

 **Review and extension**

1 GRAMMAR AND VOCABULARY

Correct the errors in the <u>underlined</u> words.

1 Would it be possible to view your collection, <u>the contents which</u> would be helpful for my dissertation?
   Would it be possible to view your collection, the contents of which would be helpful for my dissertation?
2 Could you confirm <u>the date in which</u> you returned to work?
3 I refer to <u>your email on which</u> you asked for some guidance.
4 We would like you to speak at our sales conference this year, <u>which details</u> haven't been announced yet.
5 I'm sure that <u>who finds my money</u> will keep it.
6 They stop the buses <u>where ever they like</u> because there are no designated bus stops.
7 Today, the global population is estimated at 7,800,000,000 people, <u>who</u> need food, drink and shelter.
8 The government is investing a lot of money in the <u>constructing</u> of new motorways.
9 More females than males are employed in the public <u>industry</u>.
10 After the offender is released, that person can <u>convict a crime</u> again.
11 One sector that is very customer-orientated is <u>retailing</u>.
12 We are a small <u>manifacturing</u> company based in South Korea.

2 WORDPOWER Idioms: Crime

Rewrite the sentences. Replace the <u>underlined</u> words with the words in the box. Make any changes needed.

get away with murder   look over one's shoulder
~~catch red-handed~~   up to no good   lay down the law

1 When I was about five, my brother <u>found me</u> stealing his chocolate. He was really angry!
   When I was about five, my brother caught me red-handed stealing his chocolate. He was really angry!
2 I always know when my nephew is <u>doing something he shouldn't</u> because he suddenly goes quiet.
3 My neighbour never punishes her children. They <u>just do whatever they like and there are no consequences</u>.
4 With children, you've got to <u>make sure they know the consequences of breaking the rules</u> right from the start.
5 Ever since she was mugged, my aunt's <u>been very nervous when she's out</u>. She's worried it will happen again.

↻ REVIEW YOUR PROGRESS

Look again at Review your progress on p. 66 of the Student's Book. How well can you do these things now?
3 = very well   2 = well   1 = not so well

I CAN ...	
talk about crime and punishment	☐
talk about job requirements and fair pay	☐
recall and speculate	☐
write an opinion essay.	☐

6A | WE ALL SEEM TO LOVE TAKING PICTURES

1 GRAMMAR
Simple and continuous verbs

a Underline the most appropriate words to complete the conversation.

A What's your current address?
B It's 191 Park Street. [1]*I stay / I'm staying* with friends until I can get my own place.
A Since when?
B [2]*I've lived / I lived* there since June.
A Have you got a degree?
B Not yet. [3]*I do / I'm doing* an online business and finance course with City University.
A How long have you [4]*done / been doing* that?
B For two years. [5]*Are you thinking / Do you think* that will make it difficult for me?
A Not at all. Some employers [6]*insist / are insisting* on a degree, but not all.
B That's good because I'll [7]*study / be studying* for two more years.
A [8]*Are you / Are you being* flexible?
B Yes, of course. Frankly, [9]*I need / I'm needing* the money, so [10]*I'm looking / I look* for anything full-time.
A OK. This company [11]*recruits / is recruiting* customer service assistants. You should give them a call.

b Match sentences 1–8 with a–h.

1 [g] My son is just two.
2 [ ] Your hair is soaking.
3 [ ] What do you think of the new manager?
4 [ ] Real Madrid were leading 2–0 at halftime.
5 [ ] The house has got too large for my parents.
6 [ ] My uncle lives in Australia.
7 [ ] What are you thinking about?
8 [ ] How long have you been with the company?

a Nothing really. I'm just daydreaming.
b Yes, but the match ended in a draw.
c She seems very bright and capable.
d In May I'll have been working here for ten years.
e It's raining and I forgot my umbrella.
f So they won't be living there much longer?
g He's being quite difficult at the moment.
h And he's coming all that way for your wedding?

2 VOCABULARY Adjectives: describing images

a Complete the words.

1 It is a very w <u>e</u> l l-c <u>o</u> m p <u>o</u> s <u>e</u> d photo, with the subject the perfect size for the background.
2 The photo of the orphan getting new shoes from the Red Cross is a very p_ _ _ _f _ l image.
3 She has clearly spent a lot of time watching people. Her photos are very o _ _ _ _ _ a _t.
4 The famous photo of the couple kissing in the streets of Paris is i _ _ _ _ c.
5 He doesn't take himself too seriously – his photos are always h_ _ _ r _us.
6 The photos taken in the Depression are b _ _ _ k – they perfectly express the mood of the time.
7 It's obviously posed and there is too much going on. It's too e_ _ b _r _ t_ for me.
8 You cannot criticise a single part of the photo. It is absolutely f_ _ w_ _ _ s.

b Underline the correct words to complete the conversation.

A What did you think of the exhibition?
B She's a brilliant photographer. The pictures are so [1]*evocative / elaborate* of the 1950s.
A They really are. Her subjects come across as very natural; there is nothing [2]*casual / elaborate* about the shots.
B I agree, and there's such variety. Some, such as the shots of the homeless people, are quite [3]*humorous, / gritty,* but then you get others that are really [4]*meaningful / playful* and make you smile.
A That's true. She definitely can't be accused of being [5]*repetitive / sensational.*
B It's amazing to think these photos were nearly lost forever. Some of her photos, like the ones of the Statue of Liberty, are very [6]*flawless / powerful*, particularly as that is itself an [7]*iconic / exotic* image. But the way it's composed with the people in the foreground makes it very [8]*meaningful / spacious.*

c ▶06.01 Listen and check.

d Underline the correct adverb of degree to complete the sentence.

1 We were amazed by her performance – it was *a little / extremely* powerful.
2 The story was *wonderfully / pretty* sensational and went viral that same day.
3 The photo painted a(n) *incredibly / wonderfully* bleak portrait of daily life during the war.
4 The colours in this painting are *rather / utterly* flawless.
5 This artist is really popular, but I think his paintings are *utterly / rather* repetitive.

6B | A PERSON WAVING FOR HELP

1 GRAMMAR Participle clauses

a Match 1–8 with a–h to make sentences.

1. [g] Noticing him across the room,
2. [ ] Around midnight, I heard the car
3. [ ] That guy speaking
4. [ ] Not having been there myself,
5. [ ] Having stuffed myself with chocolate,
6. [ ] Any buildings damaged by the storm
7. [ ] All the restaurants were packed with
8. [ ] *Vertigo* was the film

a I couldn't possibly comment.
b I felt sick to my stomach.
c will be assessed for insurance purposes.
d tourists eating the local speciality.
e selected by most critics as the best ever.
f is my dad.
g I went over to introduce myself.
h coming slowly down the street.

b Complete the extract from a crime novel with the words in the box.

> brushing   frightened   crackling   having completed
> sensing   waiting   ~~having taken~~   pausing   looking
> having considered

¹<u>Having taken</u> off his overcoat, the detective strolled into the living room ²_____ calm and confident. The guests were sitting quietly, ³_____ for his explanation of the terrible incidents. ⁴_____ for a second, he looked around the room. All was quiet except for the sound of the fire ⁵_____ in the fireplace. ⁶_____ some invisible dust off his sleeve, he began to talk. 'Someone in this room saw the murder but, ⁷_____ by what they saw, they refuse to speak.' ⁸_____ he had the attention of the room, he continued. 'Everyone in this room had a motive to kill Mr Kushner, but ⁹_____ all the evidence, I now know for sure who did it.' ¹⁰_____ his opening speech, he turned to Melissa …

2 VOCABULARY Emotions

a Match sentences 1–8 with their continuations a–h.

1. [c] I thought I should try bungee jumping.
2. [ ] She decided to leave home at 16.
3. [ ] It was such an amazing surprise.
4. [ ] He never appears calm or relaxed.
5. [ ] Nothing I tried last year seemed to work.
6. [ ] The job wasn't at all what she had been expecting.
7. [ ] Most of my colleagues had a lot more experience than I did.
8. [ ] He's good-looking, popular and successful.

a I got very frustrated.
b Most of us are extremely jealous.
c As I waited, I was absolutely petrified.
d I was a bit insecure.
e Her family were absolutely devastated.
f I was totally speechless.
g She felt completely disillusioned.
h He's always very restless.

b Complete the sentences with the words in the box.

> ~~petrified~~   frustrated   satisfied   overexcited
> ashamed   overjoyed   insecure   jealous

1. He was __*petrified*__ at the thought of having to make a speech in front of so many people.
2. I feel so _____ of myself for reacting so rudely.
3. It's normal to feel anxious and _____ when meeting people for the first time.
4. He was extremely _____ of his colleague, who was promoted ahead of him.
5. Her parents were _____ at the idea of their daughter going to one of the best universities in the country.
6. My classmate had a very _____ smile on his face when he found out he came top in the exam.
7. Too many sugary drinks can get children _____.
8. She got very _____ by the number of rejection letters she received.

3 PRONUNCIATION Emphatic stress

a ▶ 06.02 Listen and <u>underline</u> the stressed word in each sentence.

1. She was <u>so</u> disillusioned.
2. She was so disillusioned.
3. I was absolutely petrified.
4. I was absolutely petrified.
5. I felt extremely frustrated.
6. I felt extremely frustrated.
7. They were very jealous.
8. They were very jealous.
9. I'm really ashamed.
10. I'm really ashamed.

6C EVERYDAY ENGLISH
First and foremost

1 USEFUL LANGUAGE
Organising a presentation

a Match the underlined expressions in sentences 1–12 with their functions a–e. Sometimes more than one answer is possible.

1 <u>First and foremost</u>, we need to look at the sales.
2 <u>I am here today</u> to talk about development.
3 <u>If that is all clear, let's move on</u> to finance.
4 <u>If you'd like me to elaborate</u> on that, I can.
5 <u>Let me take you through</u> that in more detail.
6 <u>Let me talk you through</u> that with an example.
7 <u>So to recap</u> what I have been saying …
8 <u>Turning now</u> to our future plans …
9 Now, <u>does anyone have any questions?</u>
10 <u>One thing is clear</u>, it is a very large market.
11 <u>More specifically</u>, we need to look at this area here.
12 <u>My focus today is</u> on Thailand.

a ☐ ☐ Introducing the presentation topic
b ☐ ☐ Changing focus
c ☐ ☐ ☐ ☐ Going into detail
d ☐ ☐ ☐ Summarising and inviting questions
e ☐1☐ ☐ ☐ Highlighting a main point

b Complete the sentences from a presentation with the words in the box.

~~focus~~   elaborate   in conclusion   first and foremost
perfectly obvious   talk   perspective   moving on
recap   table   specifically   is clear   take   turn

1 Thanks very much for your warm welcome. My
___focus___ today is regional development with a
particular emphasis on Latin America.
2 One thing _____: we really need to have a larger
presence in this region if we wish to increase our market
share.
3 _____, I would like to give you some statistics
about the country, which will put things into _____.
4 It's _____ that, with a market this size, we need
good distribution, and that is one of the areas I would
like to _____ you through.
5 _____ from distribution, let's now _____
to finance and look at the numbers.
6 This _____ shows the population by age and
area, and I would like to _____ you through it in
some detail.
7 So _____, this is the region I feel we should
concentrate on – more _____, these two cities.
8 So to _____ what I've been saying, this is a
great opportunity and I would like to offer my full support
for this initiative.
9 If you'd like me to _____ on anything, please let
me know.

c ▶06.03 Listen and check.

2 PRONUNCIATION
Intonation in comment phrases

a ▶06.04 Listen to the sentences. Does the intonation of the comment phrase rise (↗) or fall then rise (↘)?

	↗	↘
1 <u>Generally speaking</u>, the average working week is 42 hours.	✓	☐
2 Here you get four weeks' paid holiday a year <u>as a rule</u>.	☐	☐
3 <u>As a rule</u>, I'm the last to leave the office.	☐	☐
4 <u>In fact</u>, in some countries you don't get any holiday during your first six months.	☐	☐
5 I think I prefer the European system <u>on the whole</u>.	☐	☐
6 I didn't really enjoy working for that firm, <u>truth be told</u>.	☐	☐
7 <u>Normally</u>, I have two large meals a day.	☐	☐
8 <u>Actually</u>, it's a public holiday here tomorrow.	☐	☐

6D | SKILLS FOR WRITING
I enjoy helping people

1 READING

a Read the application email. Are the sentences true or false?

1 This is an unsolicited job application.
2 He is applying for a position contributing articles.
3 Thanks to his research, he has a wide range of contacts in the area.
4 His research was on the treatment of injuries.
5 The event he helped organise last summer benefited local clubs.
6 He is already working with one up-and-coming athlete.
7 If possible, he prefers working independently.
8 He writes articles already for his own interest.

b Read the email again. Match paragraphs 1–7 with summaries a–g.

a ☐ Closing lines
b ☐ A specific offer of services
c ☐ A summary of why he is a good candidate
d ☐ A description of a recent project he was involved in
e ☐ Another example of his involvement in local sports
f ☐ A factual summary of his current activity
g ☐1 A statement of why he is writing

2 WRITING SKILLS Application emails; Giving a positive impression

a <u>Underline</u> the correct words for a formal email.

¹*Dear Mr Williams, / Hi,*

²*Just a quick note / I am writing* to express an interest in the advert that ³*was / appeared* in your February issue. I think I'd ⁴*fit / match* in well at your charity as I've got extensive ⁵*work / experience*. A ⁶*neat / good* example of my charity work was my recent ⁷*running / completion* of a half-marathon, which ⁸*raised / made* £300 for a local children's hospital.

I ⁹*hope / feel* you will find my application ¹⁰*interesting / a good read*. I'm ¹¹*attaching / fixing* my CV.

¹²*Talk soon, / Kind regards,*

Laura Girelli

Document1

Dear Sir/Madam,

1 I'm writing in reply to your advert in the February issue of *The Bridge*. I'd be very interested in becoming a contributor to the magazine.

2 As a regular reader, I must say I really like the way you encourage contributions from young writers. I'd very much like to write articles about sport and other leisure activities in the area.

3 I'm currently in my third year at university, studying sports science. My dissertation is on injury prevention for young athletes and I received help with my research from a large number of local clubs. This has taught me a lot about networking. There's a wide range of sporting activities available in the area, all organised by passionate people who are keen to get wider recognition for their clubs.

4 I'm very much in touch with young athletes in the area. I played an active role organising the Junior Olympics here last summer, which over 200 children competed in. We got a lot of local press coverage and even had a short piece on the local TV news. What was rewarding about the event was that some of the lesser-known sports had an opportunity to raise their profile, and they all subsequently got new members.

5 I've also taken a keen interest in the local rowing club, helping Toby Rudd, a rower with huge potential, with his fitness programme in preparation for the national championships. I'm sure that your readers would be interested to read more about our local sporting heroes.

6 I feel that with my combination of academic studies and practical interest in sport, I'd be very well qualified to help out on your magazine. I am well organised and work well either alone or as part of a team. I'm attaching an article from my blog as an example of my writing style and a link to my online CV.

7 I'm looking forward to hearing from you.

Yours faithfully,

Deniz Tufan

Page 1 of 1   324 words   110%

3 WRITING

a Write an application email (250 words) applying for the position in the advert.

Film reviewers needed
for university magazine

ADMIT ONE

We are currently looking for contributors to write film reviews on a weekly basis.

Reviews need to be 250 words in length. Candidates should be interested in film and be capable of writing critically and engagingly. The work is unpaid, but cinema entry is free.

Remember to mention:

- your interest in the role
- your current activity
- personal strengths which would be useful
- some examples of related activities.

1 READING

a Read the article about Cindy Sherman. Tick (✓) the best summary.

1 ☐ Cindy Sherman makes extremely detailed portraits of different women in order to make us feel that society treats some of them in a way that is unfair.

2 ☐ Cindy Sherman photographs herself in a way that represents stereotypes of women in order to make viewers question their ideas about gender and status.

3 ☐ Cindy Sherman uses costumes and makeup in order to pretend to be other women so that she can photograph herself and not need to use models.

b Read the article again. Match paragraphs 1–7 with summaries a–g.

a ☐ It describes how Sherman notices small details.

b ☐ It describes the variety of her subjects.

c ☐ It explains that she only photographs herself.

d ☐1☐ It gives some biographical details.

e ☐ It talks about the people who look at her photographs.

f ☐ It mentions her childhood.

g ☐ It describes the author's reaction to seeing Sherman's photographs for the first time.

c According to the article, are the sentences true or false, or is there not enough information to be sure?

1 Sherman found photography more suited to her ideas than painting.

2 She likes to choose many different women to photograph.

3 Some of her photographs look very much like paintings.

4 She works with a team of people to create her photographs.

5 She feels sympathy for the characters in her photographs.

6 The photographs cause a wide range of emotions in viewers.

7 The women portrayed in the photos often seem familiar to us.

8 The author enjoyed Sherman's New York exhibition very much.

d Imagine you have been to a photography exhibition. Write a blog post about it. Think about these questions:

• What kind of photos were they? (Nature, action, fashion, abstract, historical?)

• What did you like about them?

• What did you dislike about them?

• Would you recommend the exhibition to other people?

The woman of many faces

1 Cindy Sherman is by no means your average photographer, but she is undoubtedly one of the most important and influential artists working today. Sherman was born in New Jersey and studied visual arts at Buffalo State College. Having started out as a painter, she quickly became frustrated with what she considered to be the limitations of the form and turned to photography instead.

2 She has now been making her strange, powerful and thought-provoking images for over thirty years, but unlike most other photographers, she has only one subject: herself. Or to be more accurate: her own body dressed up in a range of elaborate costumes designed to draw the viewer's attention to some of the most important issues of gender, status and identity that affect us today.

3 I will never forget the first time I saw a Sherman exhibition. Not knowing anything about her work, it took some time before the truth gradually dawned on me. I was amazed to realise that what looked like traditional society portraits in their grand frames were in fact photographs. Even more astonishingly, all those varied, fascinating, horrifying and moving faces belonged to the same person: the artist herself.

4 Sherman's great gift is that she is hugely observant. The detail in some of her work is astounding, and she has said that even when she sees someone walking down the street towards her, she will notice subtle things about them that most of us would miss. She then goes to enormous lengths to recreate those details, working in multiple roles as model, director, make-up artist and set designer, as well as photographer. Many of her photographs are shot with the aid of mirrors, just like the selfies of today!

5 Speaking in an interview in 2011, Sherman described how she has been dressing up all her life, ever since she was a young girl fascinated by the glamorous actresses she saw on screen. What she does now goes way beyond dressing up, though, and she is adamant that the pictures are not self-portraits. She describes herself as 'disappearing' into the characters, and it is true that she almost *becomes* the people in her photographs.

6 And what a range of characters they are! From movie stars to clowns to ageing society ladies – their personalities, their faults and their insecurities are exposed to the world, and the experience of looking at them is uncomfortable, compelling, amusing and moving all at the same time. To look at her work is to come face-to-face with society's stereotypes. These are not specific women and the photographs are deliberately untitled; nevertheless, when we look at them, we feel we know people like this.

7 Visiting a major exhibition of her work in New York's Museum of Modern Art, I couldn't help but draw comparisons between the images and some of the wealthy women walking around the gallery. Did they recognise themselves, I wondered? In many ways, I hoped not. Who wouldn't be devastated to see their own life held up for detailed examination in this way?

2 LISTENING

a ▶ **06.05** Listen to the conversation between two photographers, Lewis and Martha. Complete the sentences.

1 _____ works as a news photographer.
2 _____ works as a celebrity photographer.
3 Lewis was in an _____ in Pakistan.
4 Martha wants to go to _____ school.
5 Martha is _____ years old.

b ▶ **06.05** Listen again. Tick (✓) the correct answer.

1 Why does Lewis think Martha is doing well?
  a ☐ Her job takes her to nice places.
  b ✓ She's selling a lot of photographs.
  c ☐ She has a good job.

2 Why is Lewis jealous of Martha?
  a ☐ He thinks her job is more comfortable than his.
  b ☐ She is making a lot of money.
  c ☐ She likes her work.

3 What does Martha say is better about Lewis's job?
  a ☐ It's more interesting than hers.
  b ☐ It's easier than hers.
  c ☐ It is more worthwhile than hers.

4 Why did having a daughter change Martha's perspective on her job?
  a ☐ It made her want to have more time at home.
  b ☐ It made her more aware of issues connected to body image.
  c ☐ It made her think about how to change her life.

5 Why is Martha thinking of going to drama school?
  a ☐ Acting is something she really loves.
  b ☐ She's not successful at photography.
  c ☐ She doesn't want to be a wedding photographer.

6 What effect does their conversation have on Lewis?
  a ☐ It makes him very surprised.
  b ☐ It makes him question whether he should change jobs, too.
  c ☐ It makes him want to spend more time watching football.

c Write a conversation between two people discussing a great news photograph. Think about these questions or use ideas of your own:

• Where did they see the photograph?
• What makes it a really good news photo?
• How does it make them feel?

⊙ Review and extension

1 GRAMMAR AND VOCABULARY

Correct the errors in the underlined words.

1 Each time <u>you are doing this</u>, your English definitely gets better.
Each time you do this, your English definitely gets better.
2 The popularity of photo storage sites fluctuated over the period, but generally <u>were increasing</u>.
3 <u>Not being</u> very happy in my childhood, I tried to bring my children up differently.
4 <u>Experiencing it</u>, I must say that the way the event was reported gave the wrong impression.
5 She walked the whole night, <u>knowing not where to go</u>, what direction to take.
6 If parents do not have time to spend with their children, they will <u>get frustrate</u>.
7 People sacrifice their savings to get something that will <u>make other people jealous</u>.
8 <u>I would be devestated</u> if I ever lost my phone!
9 Lack of positive feedback can make you <u>feel unsecure</u> and lose self-confidence.
10 Although the authors describe serious problems, they do it <u>in a humoristic way</u>.

2 WORDPOWER Idioms: Feelings

Rewrite the sentences. Replace the <u>underlined</u> words with the words in the box. Make any changes needed.

grin and bear it   over the moon   get on one's nerves
can't believe one's eyes   ~~at the end of one's tether~~

1 My boss just keeps giving me more and more work. I'm exhausted. I <u>feel like I can't cope any more</u>.
My boss just keeps giving me more and more work. I'm exhausted. I'm at the end of my tether.
2 I went to a wedding last weekend and the bride's dress was bright green – I <u>was amazed</u>!
3 When I was a little girl, my parents told me we were going on a plane to visit my grandparents. I was <u>so excited</u>!
4 One of my colleagues tells jokes all the time, and they're not very funny ones. It really <u>annoys me</u>.
5 I told my friend I'd go to a dance class with her. I don't like dancing, but I'll <u>put up with it</u> if it makes her happy.

⟳ REVIEW YOUR PROGRESS

Look again at Review your progress on p. 78 of the Student's Book. How well can you do these things now?
3 = very well   2 = well   1 = not so well

I CAN ...	
describe photos and hobbies	☐
tell a descriptive narrative	☐
organise a presentation	☐
write an application email.	☐

7A | IT MUST HAVE SEEMED LIKE SCIENCE FICTION

1 GRAMMAR
Speculation and deduction

a Match sentences 1–8 with their continuations a–h.

1 [a] Wind power may well become more popular.
2 ☐ The train is running about an hour late.
3 ☐ Dusit's wearing a tie.
4 ☐ I missed your phone call.
5 ☐ I'm sure you're the best person for that job.
6 ☐ She must have studied in Australia.
7 ☐ The electric car is bound to get better in time.
8 ☐ I bet Mario will be at the conference.

a It's environmentally friendly, and that's more important to people nowadays.
b I was driving and the signal must have been bad.
c He hardly ever misses one.
d I'll be surprised if you don't get it.
e They just really need to improve the battery.
f He must be going to an interview.
g Have you heard her accent?
h We probably won't get to Bilbao before midnight.

b Complete the conversation with the words in the box.

it's likely that   should have   there's a reasonable chance
could have   bound   couldn't have   almost certainly
may well

A Hi, Lewis. Good to see you again. What are you doing here? I thought you worked in the Madrid office.
B I do, but I'm here for an interview for account executive.
A Wow. You ¹ _should have_ told me. We ² _____ met up last night.
B I had dinner with Rob. I ³ _____ prepared for the interview without his help.
A So, what are you going to tell them?
B Well … ⁴ _____ the new system will be a great improvement. We seem to be having difficulties getting paid, so the new process ⁵ _____ improve things.
A What do you think your chances are?
B Pretty good, I think. They ⁶ _____ won't give it to an external candidate, and ⁷ _____ I am the only applicant!
A Well, good luck! If you're successful, we're ⁸ _____ to be seeing more of each other.

c ▶ 07.01 Listen and check.

2 VOCABULARY Compound adjectives

a Complete the sentences with the most appropriate words in the box.

half-hearted   narrow-minded   heartbreaking
mind-boggling   hard-hearted   open-minded
heartwarming   warm-hearted

1 The kitchen was amazing, with a _mind-boggling_ range of gadgets and equipment.
2 She's so kind, friendly and sympathetic – a really _____ person.
3 The happy ending after such a hard struggle through poverty and illness was really _____.
4 He showed very little enthusiasm for the job. In fact, it was all rather _____.
5 He is never interested in other people's feelings. He is so _____.
6 Our new manager is very _____, always willing to listen to different ideas.
7 The old manager was _____ and never really listened to anyone.
8 It was _____ to see all those poor children suffering so much.

b Match adjectives 1–7 with definitions a–g.

1 [f] clearheaded
2 ☐ tongue-tied
3 ☐ hair-raising
4 ☐ backbreaking
5 ☐ mouthwatering
6 ☐ jaw-dropping
7 ☐ absent-minded

a tending to forget things
b stunningly amazing
c looking and smelling delicious
d so shy and nervous that you cannot speak
e physically very demanding
f calm and logical
g frightening and exciting

7B WHAT I ENJOY IS A HEART-TO-HEART CHAT

1 GRAMMAR Cleft sentences

a Match 1–8 with a–h to make sentences.

1 [c] The reason we chose Antalya was
2 [ ] What he suggested
3 [ ] All you can do is
4 [ ] It was at the meeting
5 [ ] What I really need now is
6 [ ] What happened to me on holiday is
7 [ ] What really annoys me
8 [ ] What went wrong was that

a was never going to work.
b I forgot to add the flour.
c because of the diving.
d is hearing people complain.
e try your very best.
f hard to describe.
g a big cup of coffee.
h that everybody got a chance to speak.

b Put the words in the correct order to make sentences.

1 happiest / is Tulum, Mexico / I've been / the place / where .
   The place where I've been happiest is Tulum, Mexico.

2 student of mine / who first told me / it was / a former / about it .
   _____

3 I wanted / on a sunny beach / was to relax / all.
   _____

4 absolutely love / is the / what I / incredible atmosphere / about it .
   _____

5 just / what is / amazing is / the locals are / how friendly .
   _____

6 and people just / go into a café / start talking to you / what happens / is you .
   _____

7 that I'm / I'm there / only when / to be / really happy / honest, it's .
   _____

8 a job there / really hard, but / annoys me is / what really / I've tried / I can't get .
   _____

2 VOCABULARY Nouns with suffixes: society and relationships

a Underline the correct words to complete the summary of an appraisal.

You have overcome the [1]*problems / nervousness / self-awareness* you felt in meetings last year and you have demonstrated this in the way you have encouraged [2]*distribution / collection / collaboration* with our other branches. You felt you were working in [3]*exclusion / isolation / liberation* last year, so we were pleased with your work on some of the group projects, where you have shown great [4]*inspiration / innovation / separation* with new approaches the company really needs. Working with others has also helped you become more [5]*anxious / liberal / tolerant* and gain new [6]*sights / prospects / perspectives*, which is always useful when working with people.

Your requests for training in communication skills show great [7]*self-interest / self-awareness / self-satisfaction* and I'm confident that will help you on future projects. I think we can look forward to next year with great [8]*optimism / pessimism / socialism*.

b Complete the sentences with the words in the box.

ostracism   distribution   selfishness
materialism   capitalism   ~~exclusion~~

1 In most countries, serious crimes are punished by some form of ___exclusion___ .
2 Certain political philosophers advocate a fairer _____ of wealth.
3 As spiritualism declines, _____ and an interest in ownership continue to grow.
4 I am afraid that _____, a complete disregard for others, is quite common these days.
5 One of the main effects of _____ is the widening of the gap between the rich and the poor.
6 Throughout history, minorities have suffered from _____ from mainstream society.

3 PRONUNCIATION Stress in cleft structures

a ▶07.02 Listen and underline the stressed word(s) in the cleft structure in **bold**.

1 **The person I'd most like to thank is** Charles.
2 **The reason I'm here is** to help you.
3 **The one thing I cannot do is** cook.
4 **What went wrong was** I lost my ticket and got fined.
5 **The main reason I cycle to work is** to save money.
6 **The only thing I ask is** that you try your best.
7 **What will happen is** someone will be waiting with your name on a sign.
8 **What they proposed was** impossible to deliver.

7C EVERYDAY ENGLISH
I was out of line

1 USEFUL LANGUAGE
Apologising and admitting fault

a Match the underlined phrases 1–5 in the conversation with Mario's exact meaning a–d.

MARIO Hi, Andy. About the other day in the meeting. ¹I don't know what came over me.

ANDY Yes, I was quite surprised by your reaction to my proposal.

MARIO I've just been so stressed recently. ²I guess I overreacted.

ANDY I think that's putting it mildly – no one's ever spoken to me like that before. It actually really upset me.

MARIO ³I was out of line. I'm just so tired, but ⁴I had no right to take it out on you.

ANDY No, you didn't, but I understand things are difficult at the moment.

MARIO Still, ⁵it was inexcusable of me.

ANDY Well, thanks for talking to me about it. Let's just forget it, shall we?

a ☐ Andy was not at fault.
b ☐1 Mario did not expect his own reaction.
c ☐ Mario thinks his reaction was too strong.
d ☐ ☐ Mario does not think his own reaction was acceptable.

b Underline the correct words to complete the conversation.

A So what do people think of this plan for a weekend hike? Will it improve staff morale?

B Who came up with that terrible idea?

A I did, along with some of the other managers.

B Sorry, maybe I was out of ¹*words / order*. But do you really think a 20-kilometre walk in the hills will improve the atmosphere? I've had it up to here with some of the recent suggestions.

A Excuse me?

B I ²*apologise / excuse*, but when will you understand that the staff want higher wages? That's all. Any other ideas dreamed up by you and your colleagues are just a waste of time.

C Steady on, John.

B Sorry, that wasn't very ³*tactful / careful* of me. I had no right to ⁴*make / take* it out on you, but the staff are unhappy.

A We know they are, but we don't need people like you interfering.

B So making constructive suggestions is interfering, is it?

A That was ⁵*incredible / inexcusable* of me. But you need to understand that simply paying people more would be a senseless waste of money.

C That's going a bit far, don't you think?

A Sorry. I don't know what ⁶*came / went* over me.

B I was only trying to help.

A Yes. I guess I ⁷*overtook / overreacted*. Again, I apologise. Now, where were we?

c ▶07.03 Listen and check.

2 PRONUNCIATION
Sound and spelling: *ou* and *ough*

a ▶07.04 Listen to the words in the box. How are the **bold** letters pronounced in each word? Complete the table with the words.

> r̶o̶u̶t̶e̶ alth**ough** br**ough**t d**ough** t**ough** b**ough**
> w**ou**ld f**ou**r ann**ou**nce th**ough**t thr**ough**
> consci**ou**s s**ou**th c**ou**ld s**ou**thern c**ough**

Sound 1 /ʊ/ (e.g. *foot*)	Sound 2 /uː/ (e.g. *suit*)	Sound 3 /aʊ/ (e.g. *how*)	Sound 4 /əʊ/ (e.g. *throw*)
	route		
Sound 5 /ɔː/ (e.g. *saw*)	**Sound 6 /ʌ/ (e.g. *but*)**	**Sound 7 /ɒ/ (e.g. *box*)**	**Sound 8 /ə/ (e.g. *method*)**

1 READING

a Read the proposal. Are the sentences true or false?

1 It's an internal report.
2 The ideas are based on scientific research.
3 Customers have specifically requested additional support.
4 The plan is going to be expensive and time-consuming.
5 The idea is to attract the public to a new website.
6 It will free up more time for developing sales prospects.

b Read the proposal again. Tick (✓) the correct answers.

1 The report outlines a plan to offer better services to … .
  a ☐ new customers
  b ✓ some existing customers
  c ☐ all existing customers

2 An example of the additional kind of services clients have requested is … .
  a ☐ conferences
  b ☐ training
  c ☐ new products

3 The plan outlined in the proposal is … .
  a ☐ time-consuming
  b ☐ very expensive
  c ☐ neither time-consuming nor expensive

4 The purpose of the website will be to provide … .
  a ☐ promotional material
  b ☐ social networking
  c ☐ up-to-date information

5 Most of the work on the website will be done by … .
  a ☐ a supplier
  b ☐ the customers
  c ☐ R&D

6 By offering this service to customers, the sales teams will need to visit them … .
  a ☐ less frequently
  b ☐ just as frequently
  c ☐ more frequently

2 WRITING SKILLS Proposals; Linking: highlighting and giving examples

a Underline the correct words to complete the sentences.

1 The disease is now on the decline in most countries, as *told by* / *detailed in* this WHO report.
2 She has made a lot of changes in her time here, *specifically* / *generally* the introduction of hot-desking.
3 We had great motivational speakers last year, *such as* / *thus* Eric Thomas, the critically acclaimed author.
4 It has been a great success with our customers, *in particular* / *like* the smaller companies.
5 The team has had a very successful season, as *reflected* / *demonstrated* by their victory in the regional tournament.
6 The project has highlighted two of your skills, *therefore* / *namely* leadership and tact.

● ● ●   Document1   C Q ⌂

Labtec Development Proposal

This proposal outlines a plan to offer our key customers a better range of services. Feedback from recent conferences has highlighted the fact that our customers expect more from us than just the products we sell them; for example, we recently received a request for scientific training. Specifically, customers have suggested that they would benefit from more information about certain areas related to the industry, and they feel that we as the supplier are in a strong position to provide it. I have identified a solution that I believe is ideal in terms of time and expense.

I suggest we develop a Community of Practice website for our key customers. It would have access codes, so only current customers would be able to benefit. The website would act as an information resource, in particular on current developments in our field, as well as offer discussion boards on topics such as export regulations, health and safety, and transport. I have found a company that specialises in building, hosting and managing such websites, as detailed in the attached quotation. Our input would be minimal, consisting of regular updates on new products, video footage from R&D and a monthly blog. The site would also help us save time in other areas. For instance, a number of customer questions would be handled by means of a FAQ section rather than by our sales teams.

Overall, I see the website as having considerable benefits, namely retaining customers and building customer loyalty, especially among the smaller companies. It will also reduce the number of visits our sales team have to make, allowing them time to prospect other potential customers. Furthermore, it will differentiate us from our competitors and set a new industry standard in terms of customer support.

I look forward to discussing this proposal in more detail with you and am confident that you'll agree it is an innovative way of trying to defend and grow our sales.

Page 1 of 1   327 words   ☰ ☰ – ——— • —— + 110%

3 WRITING

a Write a short proposal (250 words) on the following topic.

> **Class survey**
> You have been studying English for a while now. Talk to other students and your teacher about the course and prepare a short proposal on how you would like to improve things.

Remember to include information about:

- time and frequency of the class
- size and level of the class
- class activities
- self-study.

1 READING

a Read the article. Choose the correct headings a–d for each part of the article 1–4.

- a ☐ Learning to interact with others
- b ☐ Giving and getting support
- c ☐ Knowing yourself better
- d ☐ Enjoying a long life

b Read the article again. Are the sentences true or false?

1 The author believes it's possible to extend how long you live.
2 Friends can help people control their diet.
3 Children become less aggressive when they spend time with others of a similar age.
4 Small children are too young to learn how to compromise.
5 Doctors have recently discovered that living alone is bad for the health.
6 Giving people injections of cortisol will help to reduce their stress levels.
7 Early humans tended to live lonely, self-sufficient lives.
8 Men tend to look for solutions to problems rather than discussing their concerns.

c Read the article again. Tick (✓) the ideas that are mentioned.

1 ✓ Friends may warn you about forming relationships with unsuitable people.
2 ☐ If your friends behave in damaging ways, they will influence you to do the same.
3 ☐ Getting to know other people makes children think they are strange and not normal.
4 ☐ Children have to learn appropriate strategies in order to get on with their friends.
5 ☐ If you want a long life, it is more important to have friends than to give up smoking.
6 ☐ Everyone with breast cancer should join a support group.
7 ☐ The kind of support we need from our friends is different from what it was long ago.
8 ☐ Women are better than men at supporting their friends.

d Write a magazine article about the best way to make friends. Remember to include:

- why it is important to have friends
- the best places to meet new friends (think about different stages in your life)
- how to make people want to be friends with you.

Friendship and happiness
the link is stronger than you think!

If you're striving for a long and happy life, one of the most important things you can do is make friends and put effort into your friendships. Here are four compelling reasons to put friendship at the top of your priority list:

1 _____

Self-awareness is a great tool for life and nobody can help you develop that better than the friends who know you well. True friends won't be afraid to give you an honest opinion and a reality check if you need it! They are the ones who will tell you that the person you have fallen hopelessly in love with is actually a bit of an idiot, or they'll alert you to damaging behaviour, such as eating too much junk food or being unable to control your temper, and they'll support you in dealing with it.

2 _____

When we are small children, we think that everyone's family is like our own. Making friends helps us to broaden our outlook. As a result, we (hopefully!) become more open-minded and develop qualities of respect and tolerance. Another important thing we learn is how to resolve our differences. By playing with friends, young children come to realise that screaming and hitting isn't the best way to get what they want, and they learn skills like negotiating and compromising, which are of immense value later in life.

3 _____

It has been known for some time that a secure network of friends helps increase our life expectancy. Everyone knows that isolation can lead to a deterioration in mental health, but what's perhaps even more interesting is its effect on our physical health. Research tells us that as a person's social network gets smaller, their risk of mortality increases; incredibly, some studies show the correlation to be almost as strong as it is for smoking. Even cancer and heart attack patients do better if they have friends. One study showed that women with breast cancer who attended a support group had significantly better survival rates than those who did not, as well as lower levels of cortisol, the stress hormone.

4 _____

Our friends can provide valuable support to help us achieve our life goals. They will encourage us in times of self-doubt and be proud of our successes. There is almost certainly a strong evolutionary reason for this: humans are social animals who have always relied on each other for survival. Although in the past humans may have banded together to hunt for meat or gather nuts, we still benefit from the support of our friends. Interestingly, the nature of this support varies markedly between the sexes. Especially when dealing with emotional problems, women, broadly speaking, tend to be more empathetic; in other words, they are good at showing understanding. Men, on the other hand, tend to be more practical; they will be happy to mend the washing machine, but might struggle if you want to talk about your feelings!

2 LISTENING

a ▶ 07.05 Listen to the conversation. Tick (✓) the advantages of robots that are mentioned.

1. ✓ They can help with memory problems.
2. ☐ They can remind users when they need food or drink.
3. ☐ They can provide a form of friendship.
4. ☐ They help reduce the burden on existing resources.
5. ☐ They don't need any maintenance.
6. ☐ They can enable users to go outside.
7. ☐ They can benefit the person's usual carer.
8. ☐ They are easy to use by touching.
9. ☐ They can help users maintain their social lives.
10. ☐ They can do housework.

b ▶ 07.05 Listen again. Underline the correct words to complete the sentences.

1. Ingrid doesn't think that robots can *cause / help people with / understand* loneliness.
2. Carlo thinks that robots are meant to be used *in addition to / instead of / more often than* human carers.
3. Ingrid finds the idea of being spoken to by a machine very *offensive / shocking / sad*.
4. Carlo points out that existing services *can easily manage / can barely cope with / often exaggerate* the amount of work they have to do.
5. Ingrid *doesn't believe / thinks / hopes* that the government will spend any extra money on older people.
6. Ingrid thinks that using a robot might be *fun / expensive / difficult* for elderly people.
7. The robot is trained to understand the way the user *behaves / moves / speaks*.
8. Carlo *thinks / doesn't think / hopes* that robots will be able to do tasks like ironing in the near future.

c Write a conversation between two people discussing ways in which robots may be used in the future. Think about these questions or use ideas of your own:

- What kinds of things could robots do?
- Will they ever be 'intelligent'?
- Could increased use of robots lead to less personal contact between people?
- What would you most like a robot to be able to do for you?

👁 Review and extension

1 GRAMMAR AND VOCABULARY

Correct the errors in the underlined words.

1. If everyone attends, <u>it more likely</u> an agreement will be reached.
   If everyone attends, it is more likely an agreement will be reached.
2. Given previous summers, a heatwave is <u>quiet possibly</u>.
3. Skis are not <u>bound</u> to be of much use in the summer.
4. What shouldn't be <u>forgotten the</u> fact that he was born here.
5. What was <u>amazing that</u> she won the competition twice.
6. After two hours of excellent music, including <u>heartopening</u> ballads, they left the stage.
7. The risk of an accident increases when you are excited, irritated, sleepy or <u>abscent minded</u>.
8. Hotels should serve <u>mouthwatered</u> food to attract more guests.
9. In my view, animals feel <u>lonelyness</u> in the same way humans can feel it.
10. Please make sure you read the report that describes our <u>inovation</u> in data security.
11. Until his late fifties, he led his life with a fear of <u>intimity</u> and the outside world.
12. We all need warm winter clothes to protect us from the <u>coldness</u>.

2 WORDPOWER *self-*

Underline the correct words to complete the sentences.

1. I love singing, but I could never sing on stage – I'm not *self-centered / self-confident* enough.
2. She doesn't seem to realise that she's grumpy when she's hungry. She is not very *self-aware / self-satisfied*.
3. My father worked overtime to get the money to buy my first bike. He was so *self-sacrificing / self-sufficient*.
4. When I'm older, I don't want to have to rely on anyone else. I want to be completely *self-confident / self-sufficient*.
5. My brother missed our mum's birthday party because he went out with his friends. He's so *self-centered / self-aware*!

🔄 REVIEW YOUR PROGRESS

Look again at Review your progress on p. 90 of the Student's Book. How well can you do these things now?
3 = very well   2 = well   1 = not so well

I CAN ...	
speculate about inventions and technology	☐
emphasise opinions about the digital age	☐
apologise and admit fault	☐
write a proposal.	☐

8A | IT'S NO USE TRYING TO GO TO SLEEP

1 GRAMMAR Gerunds and infinitives

a Complete the text with the gerund or infinitive form of the words in the box.

> act sleepwalk create move do need
> be ~~come~~ wake up talk walk

Ever since I saw my two-year-old son ¹___coming___ downstairs at midnight, I have been interested in ²_____. It was the middle of the night, yet he appeared ³_____ awake. In fact, he was fast asleep. The following morning, he couldn't remember ⁴_____ it. He carried on ⁵_____ in his sleep until he was about ten and then he suddenly stopped. All this goes to show that you shouldn't be worried if your child starts ⁶_____ like this, but remember ⁷_____ a safe sleeping environment for them. It can also be dangerous ⁸_____ a sleepwalking child suddenly. With our son, we found it was best ⁹_____ to him and cuddle him until he woke up. Sleepwalkers tend ¹⁰_____ more sleep than other children, so ¹¹_____ bedtime a little earlier might also be helpful.

b Underline the correct words to complete the sentences.

1 *Working* / *Having worked* six days a week is killing me.
2 I wonder if it is really worth *to put* / *putting* all that effort in.
3 I'd rather *to do* / *do* something else next weekend.
4 Let me *decide* / *to decide* where we have dinner this evening.
5 What I am angry about is *not giving* / *not having been given* the chance to refuse.
6 There is still time *to alter* / *for altering* the schedule if we decide to.
7 I get so tired of *hearing* / *having heard* the same old comments.
8 I arrived home late again last night, *having waited* / *waiting* for my luggage at the airport.
9 We are sure *meeting* / *to meet* our competitors at the fair, since they always attend.
10 There is no point in *complain* / *complaining* about it if they can't change it.

2 VOCABULARY Sleep

a Complete the puzzle. What is the shaded word?

1 Someone who wakes up easily is a _____ sleeper.
2 You toss and _____ when you cannot sleep.
3 When you wake up too late, you _____.
4 A deep sleeper sleeps like a _____.
5 When you see images and imagine things happening while you are asleep, you _____.
6 It's a short sleep during the day.
7 When you are _____ awake, you cannot sleep.
8 When you are in a deep sleep, you are _____ asleep.

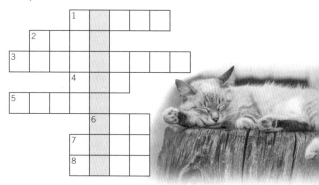

b Underline the correct words to complete the conversation.

A Oh, I'm so tired. I didn't sleep a ¹*wink* / *blink* last night!
B Really? You usually sleep like a ²*dog* / *log*, don't you?
A Yes, I'm often ³*fast* / *deep* asleep by 11.00 pm.
B That's if you haven't already drifted ⁴*off* / *on* while reading in bed!
A True. I think I'm going to have a ⁵*nap* / *tap* later.
B I can't sleep during the day. Even at night, I'm a very ⁶*slight* / *light* sleeper.
A So you find it really difficult to drop ⁷*off* / *in*?
B Oh, yes. I often just lie there ⁸*wide* / *high* awake for hours.
A Well, make sure you don't ⁹*undersleep* / *oversleep*. You've got to be up early tomorrow.

3 PRONUNCIATION Stress in fixed expressions

a ▶08.01 Listen to the fixed expressions in **bold** and underline the stressed syllables.

1 I didn't **sleep a wink** last night!
2 I usually **sleep like a log**.
3 I'm often **fast asleep** by 11.
4 I'm going to **have a nap** later.
5 I just lie there, **wide awake**.
6 Make sure you **don't oversleep**.

8B SUPPOSE YOU COULD LIVE FOREVER

1 GRAMMAR Conditionals

a Match 1–6 with a–f to make sentences.

1 ☐d If people could see the amount of sugar in certain soft drinks,
2 ☐ Had I known more about nutrition as a kid,
3 ☐ I don't eat carbohydrates
4 ☐ You can eat pretty much what you like as long as
5 ☐ I would have lost even more weight
6 ☐ Supposing I followed this diet,

a your diet is balanced.
b if I had taken up cycling earlier.
c unless I have been for a run first.
d they wouldn't buy them.
e I would be in much better condition now.
f how much weight could I expect to lose?

b Underline the correct words to complete the sentences.

1 I didn't go to the conference, _otherwise_ / unless I would have seen you.
2 Take this money _supposing_ / _just in case_ you need some.
3 You will be able to hire a car there _provided that_ / _unless_ you've got your papers.
4 _In case_ / _Assuming_ nothing else goes wrong, we will have finished by Saturday.
5 Just give me a call _should_ / _would_ anything change.
6 If it _wouldn't be_ / _weren't_ for you, I would never have heard of this place.
7 We can change the flight _on condition_ / _otherwise_ that you inform us at least 48 hours before.
8 _Suppose_ / _In case_ you could have dinner with one historical character. Who would it be?

2 VOCABULARY Ageing and health

a ▶08.02 Listen to the advert and complete the information.

Three-Step Plan to a Better Life

Are you ¹___showing___ your age? Do you have ²_____ skin, fine lines and ³_____?

Are you prone to ⁴_____ skin? Is your hair ⁵_____ and greying?

Adopt our plan to prevent those visible signs of ⁶_____.

Step 1	⁷_____ and have weekly facials to ⁸_____ and plump the skin.
Step 2	Eat a varied and ⁹_____ diet to lose ¹⁰_____ and get yourself a ¹¹_____ complexion.
Step 3	Help poor ¹²_____ and prevent ¹³_____ trouble by doing regular ¹⁴_____ exercise.

b Underline the correct words to complete the text.

Charles Eugster was a former dentist who did not ¹_show_ / _tell_ his age in the slightest. At 95, he broke the world record for running the 200 metres in the over-90 age bracket. About 15 years ago, in an attempt to improve his appearance, he didn't take the option of ²_plastic_ / _beauty_ surgery, but instead, he started training as a bodybuilder, doing regular ³_fattening_ / _strengthening_ and ⁴_tanning_ / _toning_ exercises. His skin slowly ⁵_tightened_ / _thinned_ and got ⁶_firmer_ / _fitter_ and his complexion started to ⁷_grow_ / _glow_. About five years later, he took up running, which gave him ⁸_regular_ / _usual_ cardiovascular exercise and a chance to compete. For Charles, there were three secrets to a healthy life: hard work, a varied and ⁹_light_ / _balanced_ diet and exercise. Unlike many people, he really enjoyed ageing.

3 PRONUNCIATION Pitch: extra information

a ▶08.03 Listen to a person giving instructions. Write the extra information she gives and notice the lower pitch.

1 Take your eggs, _____, and break them in a bowl.
2 Take a whisk, _____, and beat them.
3 Add some salt and pepper, _____, and stir.
4 Take some hard cheese, _____, and grate it.
5 Melt some butter, _____, in a frying pan.
6 Pour the mix – _____ – into the pan and cook for a minute or two.
7 Add the cheese and wait, _____, until it melts.
8 Serve immediately.

8C EVERYDAY ENGLISH
Is that your best offer?

1 USEFUL LANGUAGE Negotiating

a <u>Underline</u> the correct words to complete the conversation.

A How much would you be [1]<u>willing</u> / keen to pay?

B We'd be [2]prepared / preparing to offer somewhere around a hundred and eighty.

A We were kind of [3]expecting / hoping for more in the region of three hundred.

B I'm afraid that's out of [4]touch / the question. What would you [5]say / react to two forty?

A Two forty? Is that your best [6]go / offer?

B It will have to be. I'm not [7]authorised / open to go any higher.

A Could you see your [8]time / way to increasing that to two hundred and fifty?

B Possibly. There's just the [9]detail / issue of availability. I'd really need it soon.

A How [10]flexible / long can you be on that? I could possibly do Saturday.

B OK. We've got a deal. Two hundred and fifty with delivery on Saturday.

b Put the words in the correct order to make statements and questions.

1 to pay / for it / how much / the question / there's just / of / you'd like .
<u>There's just the question of how much you'd like to pay for it.</u>

2 a position / to accept / I'm not / in / anything less .
_____

3 much more / that / than / the rug / is worth .
_____

4 final / is / that / offer / your ?
_____

5 to increasing / see your way / a little / could you / that offer ?
_____

6 in the region / of $100 / hoping for / a hotel room / a night / I was .
_____

c Are 1–9 said by someone buying or selling? Tick (✓) the correct box.

		Buying	Selling
1	I'd be prepared to accept …		✓
2	I'm afraid I can't go higher than …		
3	It's worth much more than that.		
4	You won't find a car like it cheaper anywhere else.		
5	That's as high as I can go.		
6	Could you see your way to increasing that a little?		
7	That's my final offer.		
8	I was kind of hoping for …		
9	I'm not authorised to go any higher.		

d ▶08.04 Listen and check.

2 PRONUNCIATION
Intonation in implied questions

a ▶08.05 Listen. Are 1–12 statements or implied questions? Tick (✓) the correct box.

		Statement	Question
1	I was thinking about a dessert.	✓	
2	I was thinking about a dessert.		
3	You sound French to me.		
4	You sound French to me.		
5	I'm not sure if you were there last week.		
6	I'm not sure if you were there last week.		
7	I was considering a takeaway tonight.		
8	I was considering a takeaway tonight.		
9	I'm doing some work for, you know, Oxfam.		
10	I'm doing some work for, you know, Oxfam.		
11	We could go out at, say, ten.		
12	We could go out at, say, ten.		

1 READING

a Read the home page of a hotel website. Tick (✓) the correct answers.

1 The opening paragraph ... .
   a ☐ describes the hotel
   b ✓ gets the reader's attention
   c ☐ does neither of these

2 The second paragraph ... .
   a ☐ describes some of the amenities
   b ☐ asks questions
   c ☐ lists activities

3 The hotel would be a good choice for ... .
   a ☐ a large family celebration
   b ☐ a company awayday.
   c ☐ a romantic break

4 The third paragraph focuses on ... .
   a ☐ the chef
   b ☐ the restaurant
   c ☐ the food

5 The food is described as delicious and ... .
   a ☐ Swedish
   b ☐ seasonal
   c ☐ organic

6 The last paragraph offers ... .
   a ☐ a description of other amenities
   b ☐ an invitation
   c ☐ both of these

b Read the home page again. <u>Underline</u> the correct words to complete the sentences.

1 The hotel is in a beautiful setting next to a *hill / <u>river</u>*.
2 It is a fabulous place to *chill out / warm up* for the weekend.
3 The hotel offers a perfect combination of *old and new / town and country*.
4 The award-winning chef has *only recently started / worked there for a while*.
5 Both the toiletries and the vegetables are *locally sourced / organically produced*.
6 The menu has a range of mouthwatering *local / international* dishes.

☰ MENU   RESERVE

Looking for a perfect weekend in the country? Ready to walk along footpaths through beautiful rolling countryside? Keen to wind down with great meals served in a picturesque riverside setting? We have the place that was designed with you in mind.

🛏 Our magnificent 16th-century manor house has seven individually designed bedrooms, all with romantic four-poster beds, flat-screen TVs, wi-fi and stunning views over the surrounding fields. After a long walk, relax in a deep bath with our own organic toiletries before going down for dinner.

✳ For ten years, award-winning chef Simon Simpson has been delighting his customers with a mouthwatering selection of delicious dishes that combine the traditional values of locally sourced food and the flavours of contemporary cooking. Relax beneath our ancient beams, sip a relaxing drink in front of our roaring fire and eat with friends and family in our Scandinavian-style dining room. Modified on a weekly basis to reflect seasonal produce, our à la carte menu will take your breath away. Using the finest vegetables and herbs from our own organic gardens, tender meat from local farms and fresh fish arriving daily, Simon concocts superbly balanced dishes, as delicious as they are nutritious. Lovingly prepared, the food has roots in the four corners of the world, so you'll be sure to find something that delights your individual taste buds.

🏋 To end the weekend, work out in our state-of-the-art fitness centre, then relax in our Turkish steam room. Have an invigorating swim in our infinity pool or play tennis on our unique French clay court. Whatever you are looking for in a weekend away, it's waiting for you here.

2 WRITING SKILLS Promotional material; Using persuasive language

a Complete the sentences with the words in the box.

~~roaring~~	deep	stunning	lovingly	state-of-the-art	romantic

1 Take a seat in front of a ___roaring___ open fire.
2 Work out in our _____ fitness centre.
3 Relax in a _____, warm bath.
4 Taste our _____ prepared dishes.
5 All our rooms have _____ views.
6 Have a _____, candlelit dinner in our dining room.

3 WRITING

a Imagine a hotel, restaurant or café. Write four paragraphs to describe it on a website designed to encourage people to go there. Think about what kind of people you want to attract as customers. Use this plan to help you:

1 Get your reader's attention.
2 Describe the place generally.
3 Go into more detail about the rooms, the food, the attractions, etc.
4 An invitation or other call to action.

1 READING

a Read the article about extreme sports. Complete the summary of the article with the correct form of the verbs in the box.

> use   say   force   accompany   ~~climb~~
> find   hang   experience   spend

¹ _Climbing_ a large rock face can take several days, so climbers are sometimes ² _____ to camp in tents that ³ _____ from the side of the rock. Although most of us would ⁴ _____ the idea terrifying, climbers ⁵ _____ that it is much less frightening than the actual climb. Ordinary people who are interested in ⁶ _____ the thrill of sleeping on a Portaledge can ⁷ _____ the services of adventure holiday companies. These companies provide instructors to ⁸ _____ paying customers on their climb and ⁹ _____ the night with them.

b According to the article, are the sentences true or false, or is there not enough information to be sure?

1 Climbing a vertical rock face uses a lot of physical and mental energy.
2 Portaledges are extremely light in weight.
3 Tommy Caldwell and Kevin Jorgeson were successful in climbing the Dawn Wall.
4 For some climbs, camping with a Portaledge is the only option.
5 Cory Rich usually worries that his Portaledge might not be attached well enough to the rock.
6 Falling ice and rocks have killed or injured several people sleeping on Portaledges.
7 Using a Portaledge in a tree is not at all exciting.
8 Holiday companies charge a lot of money for the experience of sleeping in a Portaledge.

c Write an advert for a holiday company which specialises in unusual places to stay. Use this plan to help you or use ideas of your own:

- Describe some of the places your company offers (e.g., tree houses, ice hotels, underwater or underground rooms)
- Give some details of the sleeping experiences: which are good for deep sleep, which offer a stunning view, etc.
- Include some quotes from satisfied customers.

Hanging on for a good night's sleep

Imagine your dream holiday: a lazy day on a white sandy beach, a quick swim in the turquoise water, a delicious evening meal and drifting off to sleep in a soft, clean bed.

Now imagine spending hours making your way inch by inch up a sheer rock face, your muscles screaming for mercy and your brain almost exploding from the concentration required. And then, if you can, imagine that rather than descending to recover in comfort, you hang a tiny platform made from aluminium and canvas from the vertical side of your mountain and sleep there instead, hundreds of feet above the ground.

Sounds crazy? Well, to most people, it is; but for Tommy Caldwell and Kevin Jorgeson, the first climbers to conquer the infamous Dawn Wall in California's Yosemite National Park, the sleeping arrangements that fascinated and appalled the public were the least of their worries. As they later explained, sleeping inside their hanging tents is much less scary than climbing outside them!

This kind of extreme camping is far from unique among so-called big-wall climbers, who actually have no alternative since their ascents may take days or even weeks. Adventure photographer Cory Rich, who has himself climbed sections of the Dawn Wall, describes it as the 'ultimate camping location', and insists that after a hard day's climb, he sleeps like a log. As long as he is satisfied that his Portaledge, as the portable sleeping platforms are called, is securely fastened to the rock, he finds it easy to drop off to sleep.

Even restless sleepers do not need to worry, since they wear a harness at all times to stop them from rolling over the edge of their platforms. However, harnesses offer no protection from the other hazard: falling ice and rocks. Another photographer, Gordon Wiltsie, describes climbing in the Arctic spring and seeing a lump of ice the size of a car hurtling past his bed. If it had hit him, it would certainly have been fatal.

Of course, you need to be very experienced to undertake these sorts of climbs, but for the ordinary person who craves the experience of sleeping suspended high above the ground, there are now holiday companies which can make that possible. One such firm, based in the German Alps, offers different levels of adventure. The lower levels involve tents hung from trees, which may sound tame until you learn that a) you need to climb a rope to reach them and b) they are exposed to the weather and can swing around alarmingly in high winds.

At the upper end of the scale, customers pay a substantial fee for the privilege of spending the day climbing with an instructor and then sleeping alongside them in a Portaledge at night. One customer, reviewing the experience, admitted that she didn't sleep a wink, but described watching the sun rising in the morning as one of the most amazing experiences of her life.

2 LISTENING

a ▶ **08.06** Listen to the conversation. Complete the sentences with the correct numbers.

1 Ralf will be _____ years old on his next birthday.
2 He and his wife look after _____ of their grandchildren.
3 He says that people stop being appreciated when they are over _____.
4 Maria's friend is _____ years old.

b ▶ **08.06** Listen again. Underline the correct words to complete the sentences.

1 Ralf is very *positive / anxious / negative* about his age.
2 Maria thinks he is lucky to have *so many grandchildren / good health / time to do what he wants.*
3 Maria says that older people do a lot of work *they don't want to do / in the home / without payment.*
4 Ralf's son *takes for granted / appreciates / doesn't realise* what Ralf and his wife do for him.
5 Maria's friend *has decided / doesn't want / may decide* to have plastic surgery.
6 Maria thinks that Ralf is behaving like a stereotypical *forgetful / bad-tempered / confused* old man.

c ▶ **08.06** Listen again. Tick (✓) the correct definition for each expression, as used in the conversation.

1 count your blessings
  a ☐ to wish you had more good things in your life
  b ✓ to be grateful for the good things in your life
  c ☐ to have had a very good life

2 ageism
  a ☐ unfair advantages for old people because of their age
  b ☐ unfair treatment of young people because of their age
  c ☐ unfair treatment of old people because of their age

3 be a handful
  a ☐ to be difficult to control
  b ☐ to be too little of something
  c ☐ to cost a lot of money

4 grind to a halt
  a ☐ to divide something into small pieces
  b ☐ to be in a very difficult situation
  c ☐ to be unable to function

5 on the rubbish heap
  a ☐ of very poor quality
  b ☐ no longer valued
  c ☐ no longer able to function

6 I couldn't believe my ears!
  a ☐ I was unable to hear clearly.
  b ☐ I was very surprised.
  c ☐ I didn't understand what was said.

d Write a conversation between two people discussing the advantages and disadvantages of ageing. Think about these ideas or use ideas of your own:

- health
- financial situation
- family responsibilities
- free time
- wisdom and experience.

◉ Review and extension

1 GRAMMAR AND VOCABULARY

Correct the errors in the underlined words.

1 We were looking forward to relaxing and <u>swim</u> in the sea.
We were looking forward to relaxing and swimming in the sea.
2 I am sure you are as happy as I am <u>to working</u> on this project.
3 Do not get stressed, <u>otherways</u> your performance will deteriorate further.
4 Wow! You're off to NYC! <u>If I have had enough money, I'd have come</u> with you.
5 I love that place! <u>In case,</u> I have children one day, I will take them there.
6 If I were to watch that series, <u>it'll take me</u> months to catch up.
7 The whole department needs to work on better <u>ways of communication</u>.
8 <u>Appreciated</u> is very important. Money cannot buy this feeling.
9 I'm worried that I'll <u>come out in</u> wrinkles when I get older.
10 After eating the peanuts, she <u>came out through</u> a rash.
11 Regular moisturising is a good way of <u>avoiding</u> dry skin.
12 As you age, your skin loses its firmness and gets <u>smooth</u>.
13 He's losing his hair. He's really <u>telling</u> his age.

2 WORDPOWER *and*

Rewrite the sentences. Replace the underlined words with the words in the box. Make any changes needed.

bits and pieces	~~far and wide~~	far and away
sick and tired	wear and tear	

1 The speakers at the conference came from <u>many places</u>.
The speakers at the conference came from far and wide.
2 I've just started ballet classes. They're supposed to be for adult beginners, but I'm <u>easily</u> the worst there!
3 The doctor says the pain in my knee is from <u>damage caused by everyday use</u>, so there's not much he can do.
4 I didn't do much last weekend – just <u>small tasks</u> around the house, like vacuuming.
5 My children argue all the time. I'm <u>getting really annoyed about</u> it.

◌ REVIEW YOUR PROGRESS

Look again at Review your progress on p. 102 of the Student's Book. How well can you do these things now?
3 = very well   2 = well   1 = not so well

I CAN ...	
describe sleeping habits and routines	☐
talk about lifestyles and life expectancy	☐
negotiate the price of a product or service	☐
write promotional material.	☐

9A | THEY JUST NEED TO RENOVATE IT

1 GRAMMAR
Reflexive and reciprocal pronouns

a Complete the sentences with the words in the box.

ourselves   herself   yourself   myself   one another's
~~each other~~   themselves   himself   yourselves

1 My grandparents often look at _each other_ in a very caring way.
2 All my colleagues were busy, so I had to complete the project by _____.
3 Look after _____, Maria. You don't want that cold to turn into an infection.
4 My daughter injured _____ quite badly snowboarding last winter.
5 Everyone was busy, so the man just helped _____ to a second cup of coffee.
6 Team members should be aware of _____ strengths and weaknesses.
7 We looked at _____ in the photo and burst out laughing.
8 The only advice I can give you all is to just be _____.
9 My parents think of _____ as liberal, but I find them quite strict.

b Underline the correct words to complete the sentences.

1 We spent the first session getting to know *one another* / *ourselves*.
2 After the humiliating home defeat, the coach was beside *him* / *himself*.
3 The two leaders greeted *each other* / *themselves* warmly.
4 Before the interview, I spent about 15 minutes *relaxing* / *relaxing myself*.
5 The children cooked lunch today all *by themselves* / *by them*.
6 My manager was the only person I knew, so I sat down beside *her* / *herself*.
7 My wife and I bought *each other* / *ourselves* gifts for our wedding anniversary.
8 Nobody was at home when I arrived last night, so I let *me* / *myself* in.

2 VOCABULARY Verbs with *re-*

a Complete the sentences with the correct form of the verbs in the box. There may be more than one possible answer.

recreate   regain   redevelop   regenerate
~~re-establish~~   rejuvenate   restore   renovate

1 Only a month after returning to work, she _re-established_ herself as our top sales manager.
2 After such a long illness, it took a long time for him to _____ his energy.
3 The play _____ the events that took place more than 50 years before.
4 Her job is to _____ old paintings to the way they looked originally.
5 The money will be used to _____ the commercial area damaged by the flooding.
6 His new job seems to have _____ him. He is looking and acting so much younger.
7 The city has plans to _____ the inner-city area with new roads and houses.
8 The old hotel is currently being _____. The architect's plans look very contemporary.

b ▶09.01 Listen to the report. Then complete the sentences using the correct form of the words in brackets.

1 The old Wellington waterfront needed to be _regenerated_ (regenerate).
2 The waterfront area had already been _____ (restore) three times before over the past 100 years.
3 Initially, there were a number of options for _____ (redevelop) the area.
4 After the _____, (renovate) it was important that the area be used for both work and recreation.
5 One of the main goals was to _____ (re-establish) the area as a key central location.
6 The completion of the project has made the city feel completely _____ (rejuvenate).
7 A former wetland was _____ (recreate) on the waterfront, creating habitats for ducks and other wildlife.
8 Since then, Wellington _____ (regain) its position as a tourism destination.

9B | THEY WANTED A DRAMATIC SKYLINE AND THEY GOT ONE

1 GRAMMAR Ellipsis and substitution

a Underline the briefest way it is possible to complete the sentences.

1 They played the first set faster than *the second* / *they played the second* / *the second set*.
2 He played for Galatasaray and *then Newcastle* / *played next for Newcastle* / *did for Newcastle*.
3 He said he would give me a lift, but he *never did* / *never would* / *never had*.
4 The first two years here were good, but the next two *were not so* / *weren't* / *not*.
5 I've visited many countries, but *I've visited never* / *never visited* / *never* Canada.
6 I wanted to go to Laos on holiday, but my wife *wasn't* / *didn't* / *didn't want*.

b Match questions and statements 1–6 with responses a–f.

1 [d] I'm going to have the pasta.
2 [ ] Who's got some golf clubs I can borrow?
3 [ ] Are we going the right way?
4 [ ] I don't really like opera.
5 [ ] Sarah's had another baby.
6 [ ] I hope you get home in time.

a Neither do I.
b I have.
c If I don't, I'll give you a call.
d So am I.
e I think so.
f Is that her third?

2 VOCABULARY Describing buildings

a Underline the correct words to complete the conversation.

ANDREW I hear there's a plan to renovate the old power station as part of the redevelopment project.

CARA That's right. That part of the town has been looking ¹*dated* / *timed* for years. The new design looks really interesting, and turning the power station into both flats and a museum is really ²*innovative* / *imposing* – I haven't seen that before. It will really stand out next to that ³*out-of-place* / *nondescript* retail park, which has nothing remotely interesting about it.

ANDREW What about the warehouse development that's just been completed?

CARA Well, it's great to have studios for single people to live in, though I'm not so sure about the gold balconies on the penthouses! That's a bit ⁴*stunning* / *over the top* in my opinion – kind of ⁵*tasteful* / *tasteless*, to be honest. Otherwise the design is beautiful.

ANDREW Yes, the design is certainly more ⁶*graceful* / *bland* than that massive new hotel in the town centre that seems totally ⁷*innovative* / *out of place*. It's right next to the cathedral, which looks very odd.

CARA It might be in the wrong location, but I find it rather ⁸*imposing* / *improving*, the way it dominates the old part of town. And the views from the top are simply ⁹*dull* / *stunning*.

b Complete the crossword puzzle.

→ **Across**
4 an area of land which contains many homes built at about the same time
7 a large, impressive house
9 a large building used for storage
10 a small flat with one main room

↓ **Down**
1 a house all on one floor with no stairs
2 a small house usually found in rural areas and often made of wood
3 electricity is produced in a _____ station
5 an extremely tall city building
6 joined to another similar house on only one side
8 an expensive flat or set of rooms at the top of a hotel or tall building

3 PRONUNCIATION Word stress

a ▶ 09.02 Listen to the words in the box. What stress pattern do they have? Complete the table with the words.

cabin apartment penthouse skyscraper mansion tasteless nondescript graceful innovative imposing stunning power

Oo	oOo	Ooo	Oooo
cabin			

9C EVERYDAY ENGLISH
Let's not jump to conclusions

1 USEFUL LANGUAGE
Dealing with conflict

a <u>Underline</u> the correct words to complete the conversation.

TONY Is that you, Sophie?

SOPHIE Yes, it is. How can I help?

TONY This is Tony Allen from GK Partners. I'm calling to express my utter [1]*misunderstanding* / <u>*disbelief*</u>.

SOPHIE What seems to be the problem, Tony?

TONY How can I put this? I understand you are in talks with our main competitor.

SOPHIE Well, I'm not, but a colleague is.

TONY I'm [2]*absolutely* / *very* lost for words.

SOPHIE What can I say? I take [3]*utter* / *full* responsibility, but you mustn't overreact.

TONY This is [4]*above* / *beyond* belief. I thought we had an agreement.

SOPHIE Let's not [5]*run* / *jump* to any conclusions. We are simply talking to them – that is all.

TONY But you have no [6]*duty* / *right* to work with both of us. What [7]*on earth* / *the world* happened to our confidentiality agreement?

SOPHIE There's no reason to [8]*shout* / *raise* your voice. I'm sure we can find a solution.

TONY You'd better, otherwise there will be [9]*results* / *consequences*.

SOPHIE I understand where you're coming from. I will [10]*investigate* / *study* and get straight back to you.

b ▶09.03 Listen and check.

c Put the words in the correct order to make complaints or responses to complaints.

1 let's / not / to / conclusions / jump .
<u>Let's not jump to conclusions.</u>

2 investigating / matter / have / intention / of / every / the / I .
_____

3 no / to / reason / voice / there's / your / raise .
_____

4 owe / an / me / explanation / you .
_____

5 I / consequences / you / there / will / warn / be .
_____

6 cannot / disbelief / my / utter / words / express .
_____

7 you / like / responsibility / to / I'd / full / take .
_____

8 failed / your / you've / to / responsibilities / fulfil .
_____

2 PRONUNCIATION Sound and spelling: foreign words in English

a ▶09.04 Listen to the words in the first box. Match each word to the language it comes from in the second box. Complete the table.

| abseil | baguette | cello | mosquito |

| French | German | Spanish | Italian |

Word	Original language	Meaning
1		use a rope to go down a steep slope
2		a long stick of white bread
3		a wooden musical instrument with four strings and a bow
4		a small flying insect that bites people and animals

9D | SKILLS FOR WRITING
The impact on cities is plain to see

1 READING

a Read the essay. Tick (✓) the correct answers.

1 The opening paragraph … .
   a ☐ introduces the topic
   b ☐ gives examples
   c ✓ does both of these

2 The second paragraph is mainly about … .
   a ☐ changes in shipping
   b ☐ the decline of the docklands
   c ☐ a solution

3 Migration from the docklands had led to … .
   a ☐ poverty
   b ☐ homelessness
   c ☐ an increase in crime

4 The fourth paragraph focuses on … .
   a ☐ an example of regeneration
   b ☐ statistics
   c ☐ the process

5 Tourists … .
   a ☐ attend events
   b ☐ visit cities
   c ☐ both attend events and visit cities

6 The last paragraph offers … .
   a ☐ the writer's standpoint
   b ☐ another example
   c ☐ a plan

b Read the essay again. Are the sentences true or false?

1 The decline of urban docklands is a direct result of modern shipping requirements.
2 These days, crew members are in port longer spending money.
3 Run-down dockland areas have high crime figures.
4 The Barcelona regeneration was mainly for tourists.
5 Barcelona handled the planning stages well.
6 Overall, the writer is not in favour of regenerating dockland areas.

2 WRITING SKILLS Discussion essays; Linking: reason and result

a Underline the correct words to complete the sentences.

1 The growth in the container industry has been a key *factor* / *issue* in the decline of certain docklands.
2 Container ships are getting larger and, *because of this,* / *the reason for this* they require much bigger docks to berth at.
3 *Because* / *Due to* the increase in the size of the ships, larger and more efficient cranes are needed.
4 *As a result of* / *Result of* the automation of loading, fewer manual workers are employed.
5 The regeneration of the port in Barcelona *led to* / *resulted* an increase in the number of tourists.
6 *Thus,* / *Thereby,* restaurants, cafés and cinemas have done well as a result of the redevelopment.

All over the world, from Los Angeles to Sydney, coastal cities are facing the same issue: the regeneration of their docklands. These areas, which were once at the very heart of urban activity, have emptied over time as modern shipping requirements have moved the docks further out of town. The resultant migration of population and decline in commercial activity are two effects that need to be addressed.

A key factor has been the growth of the container industry, now responsible for over 75% of goods transported worldwide. As a consequence of this, ships have progressively increased in size to such a degree that larger docks are required with more sophisticated and efficient cranes. This has led to the decline of city centre docks along with the services and homes connected to them. Another direct result is that ships spend less time in port; thus, there are fewer crew members spending money in these areas. One alternative source of revenue is the cruise industry. A number of cities are building facilities for cruise liners, which can bring over 5,000 tourists into a place in one day.

As a result of this migration from waterfront areas, hundreds of acres of land have been left to waste away. In some cities, this has meant an increase in crime in these parts as gangs have taken control and squatters have taken up residence. As the situation has got worse, the appeal of these areas for locals or tourists has decreased. This vicious circle can only be broken through redevelopment.

As a consequence, governments have had to make important financial and strategic decisions about these waterfronts, regardless of whether they open into a river, lake, bay or the sea. In Barcelona, for example, the decision was taken to regenerate the port as part of the preparation for the 1992 Olympics. Abandoned factories and warehouses were redeveloped to create a stunning destination for residents and tourists alike, with a cinema, an aquarium, shops and restaurants, and lovely public spaces open to the harbour. This meant that all the services and infrastructure required for these attractions had to be put in place. I think the statistics attached prove that the project was a great success, due in part to the consultation and planning stages, which led to a unified plan.

In conclusion, I would state that although it is sad to see the decline of such important historical waterfront areas, the resulting renovation and refurbishment can lead to economic and social improvements of great value. Therefore, I would strongly advocate regeneration plans that bring services, activity and people back to these wastelands, thereby restoring their important role in the city.

Page 1 of 1   425 words   110%

3 WRITING

a Think about a city or a town you know. Describe some redevelopment that has happened or could happen. Use these questions and the plan to help you:

- Why did or does the area require redevelopment?
- How was it or will it be redeveloped?
- What have been or will be the long-term benefits?
- Are there or were there any risks to the success of the development?

Plan:

1 Introduction
2 Benefits
3 Risks
4 Conclusion

1 READING

a Read the article. Match paragraphs 1–6 with summaries a–f.

- a ☐ It describes the specific legislation that controls the limits of the city.
- b ☐ It describes Portland's residents' love of products from their own region.
- c ☐ It describes Portland's environmental status.
- d ☐ It talks about allowing people to live near their work.
- e ☐1☐ It describes the effect of urban planning on Portland.
- f ☐ It talks about the street food stalls.

b Read the article again. Tick (✓) the correct answers.

1 Using urban planners in 1903 was … .
- a ☐ quite common
- b ☐ a good idea
- c ✓ very unusual

2 Compared to Portland, most cities … .
- a ☐ are allowed to spread out more
- b ☐ have more public transport
- c ☐ are more untidy

3 The UGB means that people in Portland can't build … .
- a ☐ high-density housing
- b ☐ new homes
- c ☐ housing on farmland

4 The city council is trying to … .
- a ☐ improve the climate
- b ☐ carry out effective environmental policies
- c ☐ take good care of the city's parks

5 The city's food stalls do not … .
- a ☐ look particularly impressive
- b ☐ serve local food
- c ☐ have enough room to operate

6 A lot of US cities are … .
- a ☐ losing population
- b ☐ starting to look alike
- c ☐ trying to copy Portland

c According to the article, are the sentences true or false?

1 Portland no longer uses steam trains.
2 The area defined by the UGB has not changed since 1979.
3 The city centre used to be deserted in the evenings.
4 Portland is more environmentally friendly than Reykjavik.
5 It is easier to walk than to drive in the centre of Portland.
6 The food stalls fit in well with the surrounding architecture.

d Write a short opinion piece about urban planning in a town or city you know well. Include the following:

- a basic description of the town or city
- what you know or can guess about how it has been planned
- which aspects of planning you think are successful
- which aspects are unsuccessful
- what improvements you would like to see.

URBAN PLANNING AND THE 'WEIRD' CITY

1 The city of Portland, in the northwest of the USA, is widely admired for a reason that may initially sound dull, but actually has a profound impact on the lives of its residents: its urban planning. In a move that was highly innovative at the time, the city employed urban planners as far back as 1903. Consequently, instead of the messy sprawl of a typical American city which results in an overdependence on cars, Portland has become a compact and contained unit with a highly developed system of public transport. It even boasts the only functioning steam locomotives in a US city!

2 Central to the character of Portland is its urban growth boundary (UGB), a planning regulation which came into force in 1979 and strictly limits development, distinguishing clearly between areas where high-density housing is permitted and agricultural areas where it is not. Although the UGB has been extended once, it does ensure that any urban expansion is the result of a conscious decision by residents themselves, and not the random growth seen in many other US cities.

3 Another major factor in the shaping of the city was the decision made by the city authorities in 1972 to regenerate the city centre. Before then, it would empty at 5 pm every day when workers left for home. Three main zones were redeveloped and thousands of new housing units were built, all of which contributed to a dramatic change in the character of the entire area, including a rejuvenation of the city's cultural and artistic life.

4 Portland is built near the point where two major rivers meet. It is a city of bridges and it looks especially stunning at night. In another bold move, the city council adopted an ambitious climate action plan in 2009, and some say that only Reykjavik in Iceland can now claim to be a greener city. Portland's over 10,000 acres of public parks are well cared for, and the revamped city centre is geared far more towards pedestrians than cars, a fact that encourages its famous street food scene.

5 The 600-plus food carts may look somewhat out of place among the skyscrapers and modern buildings, but they are one of Portland's main attractions. From these rather nondescript stalls (known as 'pods') comes the mouthwatering selection of dishes from all over the world that has made the city a foodie's paradise.

6 In fact, one of the most striking things about Portland is its focus on local consumption: a lot of the city's food comes from the farms around its perimeter. Compared with other places, it appears less affected by the seemingly unstoppable drift to sameness. You could say that Portland has deliberately associated itself with a particular, slightly alternative lifestyle, and it is probably this that gives rise to the city's proud but unofficial slogan: 'Keep Portland weird.'

2 LISTENING

a ▶️ 09.05 Listen to the conversation between Ben and Eva. Tick (✓) the best summary.

1 ☐ Ben and Eva are talking about some new apartment blocks. Eva is very critical of the way housing is being built in the city and would prefer to see the city spread outwards a little.

2 ☐ Ben tells Eva about the new apartment blocks by the river. He thinks they are extremely attractive and would like to buy one. He is horrified by Eva's idea of building around the edges of the city.

3 ☐ Ben and Eva are discussing the urban planning of their city. They would like the council to have more control over housing policy, but Eva does not care very much because she has plans to move away.

b ▶️ 09.05 Listen again. Who says these things – Ben, Eva or neither of them? Tick (✓) the correct box.

	Ben	Eva	Neither of them
1 The area by the river looks attractive now.	✓		
2 The apartment blocks are mainly for commuters.			
3 Mixed housing is less profitable for developers.			
4 The council has government funding for any legal action it needs to take.			
5 It is important to preserve the green belt.			
6 People living near the green belt strongly oppose any building there.			
7 They would like to join the city council.			
8 They are planning to restore a house.			

c Write a conversation between two people discussing the housing situation in your country. Think about these questions or use ideas of your own:

- Is there sufficient housing in your country?
- If so, how was that achieved? If not, what is preventing housing from being built?
- Is housing (private or rented) affordable? Is it of a good standard?
- What measures could be taken to improve housing?
- How important is it to maintain green spaces in and around towns and cities?

⊙ Review and extension

1 GRAMMAR AND VOCABULARY

Correct the errors in the underlined words.

1 Thanks for letting me stay with you during my time in Melbourne. I really felt myself part of the family.
Thanks for letting me stay with you during my time in Melbourne. I really felt part of the family.

2 It was a very successful event, and all the participants enjoyed.

3 We spent a lot of time this weekend just talking to ourselves about all kinds of things.

4 Look after your self while we are away and keep the house tidy.

5 I was disappointed with the film because was too long and the story was very predictable.

6 The gracefull buildings had been there for countless generations.

7 The tour was well organised, but it was a bit untasteful, like almost all package tours.

8 The results showed us that people want an innovating design, worthy of such a great city.

9 Our company wants to renew all the offices in the building.

10 We can improve the image of the city by restauring our monuments and historic buildings.

2 WORDPOWER *build*

Complete the sentences with *up, on, in,* or *around.*

1 I drink so much coffee I think I've built __up__ a tolerance to it. I seem to need to drink more every day!

2 As a business, I think we really need to build _____ our strengths – so concentrate on what we're good at and not worry about the other things.

3 My husband's parents haven't spoken to his grandparents for years. It started as a small disagreement, and then it built _____ into a huge argument.

4 I went to see a play last night. It was really interesting. The whole thing was built _____ the main character – a tall, mysterious man who walks around with a briefcase.

5 Don't forget to build _____ some time for questions and answers at the end of the session.

🔄 REVIEW YOUR PROGRESS

Look again at Review your progress on p. 114 of the Student's Book. How well can you do these things now?
3 = very well   2 = well   1 = not so well

I CAN ...	
talk about city life and urban space	☐
describe architecture and buildings	☐
deal with conflict	☐
write a discussion essay.	☐

10A | I REALLY WISH I'D BEEN ON TIME

1 GRAMMAR
Regret and criticism structures

a ▶ 10.01 Listen to the story. Are the sentences true or false?

1 His plane was late, which delayed the drive to the venue.
2 He should have arrived the day before.
3 He didn't have tea because he wanted to check his notes.
4 Luckily, he had printed out his slides.
5 The technician was good and fixed everything.
6 The room was a good size.
7 They managed to start only 30 minutes late.
8 He actually enjoyed giving the presentation in the end.

b Complete the sentences with the correct form of the verb in brackets.

1 He should _have arrived_ (arrive) the day before.
2 Had there _____ (be) less traffic, it wouldn't have taken two hours to get to the venue.
3 He should never have had tea, then he _____ (have) time to check everything.
4 He regrets _____ (print) out his slides.
5 Five minutes wouldn't have been enough had the technician _____ (be) so competent.
6 If people hadn't kept arriving, he could _____ (start) on time.
7 He really wishes _____ (give) him a larger room.
8 Things _____ (go) better, but on the whole, the presentation was a success.

2 PRONUNCIATION
Word groups and main stress

a ▶ 10.02 Listen and <u>underline</u> the stressed word in each word group.

1 If <u>only</u> she had asked me …
2 Had the weather been better …
3 I should have realised …
4 You might have told me …
5 I really wish I'd been there.
6 He ought to have known …
7 It's about time they …
8 We should never have gone.

3 VOCABULARY Communication verbs

a Match the statements and questions 1–5 with the responses a–e.

1 [d] How was the meeting? Did they present the strategy?
2 [ ] They backed up the arguments for change very convincingly.
3 [ ] Why did they need two hours to demonstrate the new approach to time management?
4 [ ] They definitely demonstrated their understanding of digital marketing, didn't they?
5 [ ] What do you think of those two who attacked the policies?

a Do you think so? I wasn't totally sold on the idea. It takes time.
b I agree. It took too long and they went into too much detail.
c Well, that's a bit strong. They were just voicing their concerns.
d Well, they didn't go into the finer points, but they definitely summarised the key ideas.
e Yes, but more examples to illustrate the concepts would have helped.

b <u>Underline</u> the correct words to complete the email.

✉ 📝 ☆ 🏳   ⊗

Hi Elaine,

Here's some feedback on the event I went to the other day.

The first speaker [1]<u>addressed</u> / spoke / approached the conference on the issue of sustainable tourism. He [2]showed / illustrated / underlined his points very well with some quotes from famous explorers, which was a unique way of doing it.

The next speaker then moved [3]away / on / out to a slightly different topic and talked about a project in Costa Rica. She [4]cleared / demonstrated / manifested a new approach to research and then [5]presented / told / had her results. The approach looks interesting, although she didn't go into all [6]the information / the finer details / a full discussion. She [7]finalised / ended up / concluded by saying more time would be needed to assess its true value. The organiser then thanked everyone there for attending and also paid [8]tribute / praise / out to Charles, who has been so influential over the years (and is now retiring).

At this point, there were one or two throwaway [9]remarks / whispers / speeches about the poor quality of the refreshments, but overall it seemed to have been a successful morning.

Thanks for giving me the opportunity to go.

Regards,
James

10B | HE IS KNOWN TO HAVE AN UNUSUAL RITUAL BEFORE HE PLAYS

1 GRAMMAR Passive reporting verbs

a Complete the text with the words in the box.

> being generally viewed   been proved   claimed
> been perceived   ~~believed~~   been said
> considered   is known   have originated   thought to

It is widely [1] _believed_ that superstition has a great influence on our lives. Scientists accept its importance, and it is actually [2]_____ that many superstitions have a factual or scientific origin. It has [3]_____ for hundreds of years, for example, that if the sky is red at night, there will be good weather the following day. It has since [4]_____ scientifically that as the sun sets it creates red light if it is shining through calm, still air.

Colours are important elements in superstition throughout the world, with the rainbow [5]_____ as a good luck symbol, either because it is a natural sign of the end of bad weather or because it is one of the few natural phenomena with the full range of colours. Scientifically, it is a fact that you cannot physically get to the end of a rainbow. This may be why it is [6]_____ to be an extremely lucky place.

White [7]_____ to represent purity in many cultures and on New Year's Eve in Brazil people wear white as it is [8]_____ bring good luck for the following year. If you are by the sea, you are also encouraged to jump the waves seven times. Both of these traditions are said to [9]_____ as acts to the goddess of the seas to bring prosperity and security, but the number seven crops up in traditions all over the world – probably because it has always [10]_____ as a perfect number, again a mathematical truth behind the superstition.

b Underline the correct words to complete the sentences.

1 All over the world, the ladybird is *being said / said / been said* to bring good luck.
2 Vikings are said to *have thought / having thought / think* of acorns as lucky charms.
3 New Year's resolutions *are / are being / have been* believed to have been introduced in Babylon.
4 In the old days, it *has been / was / was being* assumed that the Earth was flat.
5 The number eight and the colour red *are known / are being known / have known* to be symbols of good luck in China.
6 Seeing a black cat *is / has / are* thought to bring good luck in some cultures and bad luck in others.
7 Stories about the abominable snowman *have been shown / are showing / are shown* to be false.
8 In Scotland, it is *required / said / hoped* that your first visitor of the year should be tall, dark and handsome.

2 VOCABULARY Superstitions, customs and beliefs

a Complete the words.

1 **A** Good luck with your driving test. I hope you pass this time!
   B Thanks, it would definitely be a case of third time l u <u>c</u> k y though, wouldn't it?
2 **A** Aren't you going to have a second go at becoming team leader?
   B Well, I'm not sure. I think I might be tempting f _ _ _ if I tried again.
3 **A** Have you got your exam results yet?
   B No, but fingers c _ _ _ _ _ d I've been successful this time.
4 **A** That restaurant you've booked looks really expensive.
   B Don't worry, I've taken out extra cash just to be on the s _ _ _ side.
5 **A** I hear you're going skiing. Be careful you don't break anything.
   B Well, touch w _ _ _; I've been skiing for over ten years and never had an injury yet!

b ▶ 10.03 Listen and check.

c Replace the underlined words with the words in the box.

> convinced   persuasive   far-fetched
> ~~gullible~~   dubious   plausible

1 They were <u>too willing to believe what they were told</u>.
  gullible
2 She was <u>completely sure</u> he was telling the truth.
3 The story was <u>believable because it matched the facts</u>.
4 Their explanation was <u>exaggerated and difficult to believe</u>.
5 It was very <u>believable because it was well argued</u>.
6 I was <u>not sure whether to believe them or not</u>.

3 PRONUNCIATION Consonant clusters

a How many consonant clusters are there in each sentence? Write *4*, *5* or *6*.

a [6] Acorns protect you from lightning strikes.
b [ ] People claim that ladybirds bring good luck.
c [ ] The four-leaf clover is a plant which brings good fortune.
d [ ] This charm bracelet brings strength and happiness.
e [ ] I have a rabbit's foot in my sports bag.

b ▶ 10.04 Listen and check.

10C EVERYDAY ENGLISH
Before we move on

1 USEFUL LANGUAGE Turn-taking

a Complete the conversation with the words in the box.

> after you   before we go on   as I was saying   do go on
> sorry to interrupt   ~~you could start~~   speaking of   you first

A So, thanks for coming, Anthony. We were very interested in your proposal.

B So perhaps ¹ _you could start_ by …

C Sorry, but could I have a glass of water?

B Of course. Here you are.

A Now ² _____, we are very interested in your ideas and wanted to find out some more.

C Where … ?

A Please, ³ _____ …

C I was just going to ask – where would you like me to start?

A Ah, well, I understand that you train people in making presentations.

C That's true, but, ⁴ _____, can I just say that my main job is acting? I do a wide range of radio and TV shows. Theatre as well, obviously.

B ⁵ _____, but will we have seen you on TV?

C Possibly. Four or five years ago. Anyway, as I was saying, I work with politicians and business leaders to help them give more effective presentations.

A & B So how …

B Sorry, ⁶ _____.

A How do you train them?

C Well, we work a lot on posture, breathing, relaxation, some voice drills and so on.

A ⁷ _____ posture, is it an important part of the training?

C Yes, in fact we warm up with a lot of posture exercises, which allow us to have better control over our bodies. It's a technique a lot of actors use.

A Thanks. ⁸ _____.

C Where was I?

b ▶10.05 Listen and check.

c Complete the table with the words in the box.

> ~~After you.~~   Before we go on, …   As I was saying, …
> Can I ask a quick question?
> Sorry to interrupt, but …   Perhaps you could start by …
> Speaking of X, …   You first.   Where was I?

Take a turn	
Pass a turn	After you.
Signal that you want to continue	

2 PRONUNCIATION
Intonation in question tags

a ▶10.06 Listen to the questions. Is the intonation rising (↗) or falling (↘)? Tick (✓) the correct box.

	↗	↘
1 You can't give me a hand, can you?	✓	
2 It was a great film, wasn't it?		
3 He's not available, is he?		
4 That's your bag, isn't it?		
5 That wasn't your phone, was it?		
6 You can speak German, can't you?		
7 That wasn't our flight, was it?		
8 It won't hurt, will it?		
9 Your boss is coming, isn't he?		
10 It isn't time already, is it?		

REVIEWS

Not Me, directed by 50-year-old German Thomas Kuhfeldt, is an action thriller about a middle-aged Scotsman who takes on and beats people who are trying to set him up and destroy his clean-cut reputation in the process. Ned McFarlane, a retired lawyer and semi-professional kickboxer, is played by newcomer Stephen Clown. Somehow the character rings true, even though McFarlane's status as an action hero initially seems somewhat improbable. I recently killed two hours on a plane watching this film.

The film is set in the main character's home village in eastern Scotland; while the scenery is stunning, the sleepy setting reduces the impact of the action scenes. McFarlane is set up by an ex-client for a murder that happened 20 years previously, and he spends the film trying to prove his innocence. His daughter remains a close ally throughout the film, although McFarlane becomes increasingly paranoid about who is really on his side.

The fast-moving plot isn't particularly credible. McFarlane's apparently squeaky-clean, fairly uninteresting past turns out to be murkier than it first appeared, with characters from the kickboxing underworld emerging at different points in the film. McFarlane eventually seems to have enough evidence to prove that he is not the killer, but, instead of taking this to the police, he decides to trap the killer himself, with action-packed but fairly predictable consequences.

Every cliché of the genre is then enacted, including the death-defying car chase, the miraculous escape, outdoing the dim-witted villains and a finale set in a beach-side home. The stunning special effects are particularly well done.

I won't spoil the ending because if you don't guess it after about ten minutes, you really aren't concentrating. All in all, it is a very easy film to watch, and if you like black-and-white characters and unsubtle dialogue, you will have a great two hours.

1 READING

a Read the film review. Tick (✓) the information included in the review.

1. ☐ The names of most of the leading actors
2. ☐ Where the reviewer watched it
3. ☐ The location of the film
4. ☐ The reviewer's opinion about the plot
5. ☐ Why McFarlane doesn't go to the police
6. ☐ Examples of dialogue
7. ☐ How the film ends
8. ☐ The reviewer's recommendation

b Read the review again. Tick (✓) the correct answers.

1. The person who plays the main character isn't _____.
   a ☐ a good actor   b ☐ popular   c ✓ well known
2. McFarlane is a very _____ character.
   a ☐ violent   b ☐ vengeful   c ☐ believable
3. His daughter is very _____ of her father.
   a ☐ trusting   b ☐ proud   c ☐ supportive
4. His earlier life turns out to be more _____ than initially suggested.
   a ☐ boring   b ☐ complex   c ☐ interesting
5. According to the reviewer, the plot is _____.
   a ☐ hard to believe
   b ☐ easy to follow
   c ☐ full of twists and turns
6. A lot of the scenes in the film are _____ of the genre.
   a ☐ best   b ☐ tired   c ☐ typical
7. According to the reviewer, the ending is not difficult to _____.
   a ☐ believe   b ☐ guess   c ☐ remember
8. The film is recommended _____.
   a ☐ wholeheartedly
   b ☐ with certain reservations
   c ☐ very highly

2 WRITING SKILLS Film reviews; Concise description

a Rewrite the underlined words to make the sentences more concise.

1. Studio Ghibli, <u>which is a Japanese company</u>, is famous for anime films.
   Studio Ghibli, a Japanese company, is famous for anime films.
2. In *Little Women*, <u>Jo, who is independent and determined</u>, dreams of becoming a successful author.
3. <u>When he realises that</u> he has no family left, Tom Hanks's character in *News of the World* returns to find the girl he saved.
4. <u>Scarlett Johansson, who was born in New York City</u>, has filmmaking in her blood – her grandfather was a screenwriter.
5. <u>Because they have special powers</u>, The Avengers are able to defeat Thanos and save the universe.
6. *Parasite*, <u>which was released in the USA in 2019</u>, was the first non-English language film to win a Best Picture Oscar.

3 WRITING

a Write a film review. Use these questions and the plan to help you:

- What kind of film is it?
- What is the plot?
- Who are the main characters?
- What is your opinion of the film?

Plan:

1. Introduce the film.
2. Describe the characters and plot.
3. Weigh up the good and bad points.
4. Make a recommendation.

1 READING

a Read the blog post. <u>Underline</u> the correct words to complete the sentences.

1 The author *believes* / *doesn't believe* that feng shui works.
2 Her friend Rob *takes* / *doesn't take* the same view as her.
3 She thinks the claims made for *ba gua* mirrors are *realistic* / *unrealistic*.
4 She describes the dangers of pointed objects in a *sarcastic* / *serious* way.
5 The way she tried to discuss the mirrors with Rob was *polite* / *impolite*.

b Read the blog post again. Are the sentences true or false?

1 Feng shui has been used for a long time.
2 The author doesn't care at all that many people believe in it.
3 She believes that good luck charms should never be displayed in people's homes.
4 The website about *ba gua* mirrors contained warnings about using them incorrectly.

5 The author thinks you could have bad experiences from using them inside.
6 She now feels threatened by the streetlight outside her window.
7 She genuinely wants to understand Rob's beliefs about feng shui.
8 She is happy with the way their discussion about it went.
9 Rob was very polite and tactful in the way he answered.
10 He feels that being rational at all times can have negative consequences.

c Write a blog post about things that people in your country do for good luck. Think about these questions or use ideas of your own:

- How long have these good luck customs existed?
- Are they connected with specific times of the year, e.g., New Year's Day?
- Do young people do them, or only older people?
- Do you do them yourself?
- Do people really believe in them, or are they simply part of a cultural tradition?

| Latest Blog | Older Posts | About |

Notes from a rationalist

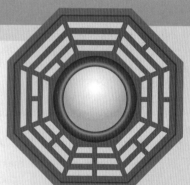

My friend Rob is really into feng shui. He honestly believes that we can improve our lives immeasurably by turning the sofa to face a different direction. Oh dear, there I go already, poking fun at my friend's deeply held belief. In fact, I'm not sure that Rob considers me a friend any more, ever since I admitted that feng shui seems like a load of far-fetched nonsense to me.

OK, let's try harder. Feng shui is – if I've understood it correctly – an ancient Chinese practice based on the idea that the way we design and arrange the direction of our buildings and their contents affects the flow of energy in a favourable or unfavourable way. It has something to do with balancing the passive 'yin' with the active 'yang' forces.

I have to admit that a lot of people take feng shui seriously, so who am I to say they are wrong? But I did find my credulity stretched to the limit again the other day when Rob told me about *ba gua* mirrors. These are placed above your front door on the outside of your house, and they're believed to both ward off evil and bring good fortune to those who enter.

I do get that. Almost every culture has similar good luck charms: horseshoes, rabbits' feet or those blue and white glass eye things you see everywhere in Greece and Turkey. I can go along with that as a bit of harmless, decorative fun. But then I went on a website that sells these *ba gua* mirrors, and I'm afraid my sceptical side was reinforced again.

'NEVER use a *ba gua* inside a house or office,' the site insists. Apparently there is a type of *ba gua* for indoor use, but this can only be sold to 'trained practitioners'.

Well, obviously you need to be highly trained; just imagine what disasters you could cause by hanging the wrong type of mirror in your living room. Oops, sorry, Rob – there I go again.

The website then explains the purpose of the *ba gua* mirror. Apparently it's to 'ward off sharp or pointed objects, such as traffic, streetlights, corners of houses pointing at you or anything that you feel is threatening'. Well, do you know what? There's a streetlight right outside my bedroom window and, until I read that, it hadn't even occurred to me to think of it as 'threatening'. Silly me, I'd thought it was there to make walking down the street safer.

I accept that I should never have said that to Rob, though. I do value our friendship, and I know we're never going to agree about this. However, another part of me is genuinely curious. It's because I respect Rob's intelligence that I'm so intrigued about how he can find this stuff plausible. Still, I really wish I'd phrased my questions more tactfully because Rob responded with some pretty frank views of his own. He said that my sneering at things I don't understand is not only insulting, but it also indicates a major shortfall in my own life. By concentrating only on what is logical and rational, he says, I'm closing myself off to much of what makes life so wonderful. Ouch.

LIKE | COMMENT | SHARE

2 LISTENING

a **10.07** Listen to the conversation between Louis and Christina. Tick (✓) the presentation topics at the conference that are mentioned.

1 ☑ Reading tasks
2 ☐ Motivating students
3 ☐ Managing behaviour in the classroom
4 ☐ Vocabulary learning
5 ☐ Improving pronunciation
6 ☐ Using digital media
7 ☐ Teaching grammar
8 ☐ Improving writing skills

b ▶ **10.07** Listen again. Tick (✓) the correct answers.

1 How does Christina feel about the conference so far?
  a ☐ She thinks it is quite interesting.
  b ☑ She rather regrets coming.
  c ☐ She can't concentrate because she is thinking about her work.

2 Christina was surprised that one of the speakers read his presentation because … .
  a ☐ presenters do not usually do that
  b ☐ he had plenty of time to learn it
  c ☐ teachers should know how to present information well

3 How did Christina feel at the end of his presentation?
  a ☐ She nearly fell asleep because she was so bored.
  b ☐ She was interested in some of the details he gave.
  c ☐ She considered leaving because she was so bored.

4 Why did Christina dislike the author's presentation?
  a ☐ She wasn't interested in her ideas on vocabulary learning.
  b ☐ Its main aim was to sell the speaker's books.
  c ☐ She couldn't understand a lot of it.

5 How does Louis feel about the presentations he has attended?
  a ☐ He now has too many ideas buzzing round in his head.
  b ☐ He has found them practical but slightly boring.
  c ☐ He has found them useful and stimulating.

6 What does Christina say about Selma Green?
  a ☐ She doesn't want to see her because she has already heard her talk.
  b ☐ She went out to dinner with her and her colleagues after her talk.
  c ☐ She is an interesting and charming speaker.

c Write a conversation between two people at a conference discussing the talks that they have heard. Think about these questions or use ideas of your own.
  • What is the theme or purpose of the conference?
  • How many speakers have they heard?
  • Who was the best speaker? Who was the worst? Why?
  • Has either of the people given a presentation at the conference? How did it go?

⊙ Review and extension

1 GRAMMAR AND VOCABULARY

Correct the errors in the underlined words.

1 I wish you can find time to meet me during my visit.
  I wish you could find time to meet me during my visit.
2 It is regarded that Pelé is the best footballer ever.
3 The price of oil was announced to be cut by 5%.
4 If only did they speak another language, they would have a more international outlook.
5 I told myself not to panic. I didn't know what I should to do.
6 I think of all the things that I would like to do but didn't have the time.
7 If I would have known that I had relatives in Dubai, I had visited you before.
8 The majority of people are absolutely persuaded that fate rules their lives.
9 In my opinion, both of the explanations were gullible. Either one could be true.
10 I recommend the Chinese restaurant in the centre of town with its typical décor and great food.
11 It's time we upgrade our conference facilities; they're really dated.
12 The information should be present objectively – I'd suggest using slides and limiting your comments to the facts.

2 WORDPOWER *luck* and *chance*

Complete the sentences with the correct form of *chance* or *luck*.

1 The players need to train a lot more to have a fighting ____chance____ of winning the game next month.
2 I get so nervous at job interviews. I'm always scared I'll blow my _____ by saying something stupid.
3 I'm working overtime every evening these days. I consider myself _____ that I don't have to work weekends, too!
4 I don't have any money to go on holiday. I need to win the lottery, but I know I don't stand a _____!
5 The shop had a special offer on laptops today. They sold out fast, but I was in _____ – I got the last one!

↻ REVIEW YOUR PROGRESS

Look again at Review your progress on p. 126 of the Student's Book. How well can you do these things now?
3 = very well   2 = well   1 = not so well

I CAN …	
give a presentation or a speech	☐
talk about superstitions and rituals	☐
take turns in more formal conversations	☐
write a film review.	☐

VOX POP VIDEO

Unit 1: Language

1a 🎥 What's your best second language?

a Watch video 1a and tick (✓) the correct answers.

1 Nora has used Spanish _____.
   a ☐ only for an exam
   b ☐ on a holiday to Costa Rica
   c ✓ for much of her life

2 Nora says Arabic _____ than Spanish.
   a ☐ is easier
   b ☐ has more similar words
   c ☐ has fewer similarities

3 Jenna thinks French _____.
   a ☐ has a lot in common with English
   b ☐ has different grammar from English
   c ☐ is just like English with a French accent

4 Ruby thinks _____ French words are similar to English.
   a ☐ all
   b ☐ no
   c ☐ many

5 _____ started learning a second language at the oldest age.
   a ☐ Nora
   b ☐ Jenna
   c ☐ Ruby

6 Both _____ talk about false friends.
   a ☐ Lauren and Ruby
   b ☐ Nora and Ruby
   c ☐ Nora and Lauren

7 All the speakers say their second language _____.
   a ☐ has difficult pronunciation
   b ☐ is similar in some ways to English
   c ☐ is easier to learn than English

1b 🎥 How important is it to know a second language?

b Watch video 1b. <u>Underline</u> the correct words to complete the sentences.

1 Nora has benefited in *one way* / *many ways* from speaking Spanish.

2 Nora thinks that foreign language books and films give you *an opportunity to learn vocabulary* / *an understanding of people in other countries*.

3 Jenna feels that when you travel abroad people often like *you to speak their language* / *to practise their English*.

4 Ruby talks about the *pleasure* / *advantages* of speaking other languages.

5 *Ruby* / *Lauren* feels it's good to learn at least a few words to use when travelling abroad.

6 All the speakers except *Jenna* / *Ruby* / *Lauren* mention the cultural benefits of knowing a language.

1c 🎥 Do you enjoy learning other languages?

c Watch video 1c. Match the speakers 1–5 with their opinions a–e.

1 [a] Lauren
2 ☐ Ruby
3 ☐ All four speakers
4 ☐ Nora
5 ☐ Jenna

a I love learning languages so much I studied them at university.
b I enjoy the feeling of achievement.
c I'm likely to stop learning a language when it gets too hard.
d The attitude to language learning in British schools is disappointing.
e Learning languages can be difficult.

Unit 2: Going to extremes

2a 🎥 Do you agree that communication isn't about what you say but how you say it?

a Watch video 2a. Match 1–6 with a–f to make sentences.

1 [c] Monika feels
2 ☐ Monika thinks
3 ☐ Laurence and Jenny think
4 ☐ Adelaide says
5 ☐ Adelaide and Jenny both say
6 ☐ Jenny probably feels

a it is easy to be misunderstood.
b modern technology can lead to misunderstandings.
c the way people from her country communicate is different.
d she has been misunderstood at work.
e the way you sound has a large impact on meaning.
f she doesn't use her hands very much when communicating.

2b 🎬 **Do you agree that good listeners make good leaders?**

b Watch video 2b and tick (✓) the correct answers.

1 Monika thinks there are other important _____ a leader needs to have.
   a ✓ qualities
   b ☐ ideas
   c ☐ qualifications

2 Graham and Adelaide agree that leaders need to _____.
   a ☐ consider what people say
   b ☐ hold people's attention
   c ☐ do what they think is right

3 According to Laurence, a good listener is _____.
   a ☐ a good leader
   b ☐ not necessarily a good leader
   c ☐ never a good leader

4 In Adelaide's opinion a leader who doesn't listen will probably _____.
   a ☐ be a success
   b ☐ not be successful
   c ☐ do what the people want

5 Jenny thinks that for leaders to make the right decisions they have to _____ different points of view.
   a ☐ ignore
   b ☐ understand
   c ☐ have

2c 🎬 **Do you agree that people who talk a lot often have the least of value to say?**

c Watch video 2c. <u>Underline</u> the correct names to complete the sentences.

1 *Graham* / <u>*Jenny*</u> finds some talkative people interesting.
2 *Graham* / *Jenny* uses a saying in giving an opinion.
3 *Adelaide* / *Graham* feels some people don't like silence.
4 Like Jenny, *Adelaide* / *Laurence* doesn't fully agree with the question.
5 *Graham* / *Laurence* uses an ex-colleague as an example.

Unit 3: Travel and adventure

3a 🎬 **Do you enjoy travelling?**

a Watch video 3a. <u>Underline</u> the correct words to complete the sentences.

1 Ruby mentions *one main reason* / <u>*several reasons*</u> she enjoys travelling.
2 Lauren loves travelling when *she is alone* / *she has free time*.
3 Only Lauren mentions activities *in the town* / *in the countryside*.
4 Jenna *likes the challenge of* / *doesn't enjoy* speaking other languages.
5 Nora would probably enjoy a holiday in a *cold* / *hot* country.
6 Nora and Jenna both talk about enjoying *galleries* / *buildings*.
7 All the interviewees mention *meeting people* / *food and cooking*.

3b 🎬 **What's the most adventurous trip you've ever been on?**

b Watch video 3b and tick (✓) the correct answers.

1 In Iceland, Ruby _____.
   a ☐ stayed in one place
   b ✓ did a lot of travelling
   c ☐ hitchhiked

2 What she enjoyed most was _____.
   a ☐ the weather
   b ☐ the wildlife
   c ☐ the scenery

3 Ruby's trip was _____.
   a ☐ frightening
   b ☐ active
   c ☐ relaxing

4 Jenna took her trip because _____.
   a ☐ she needed a change
   b ☐ she had some free time
   c ☐ she wanted to spend time with friends

5 You get the impression that Jenna's trip was _____.
   a ☐ carefully planned
   b ☐ spontaneous
   c ☐ booked well in advance

6 Jenna doesn't mention travelling by _____.
   a ☐ car
   b ☐ boat
   c ☐ bus

7 Jenna says she went to many different countries and _____.
   a ☐ ate lots of food
   b ☐ made lots of friends
   c ☐ saw lots of films

8 Jenna feels it was adventurous because she _____.
   a ☐ went to lots of places
   b ☐ went white water rafting
   c ☐ didn't go with anyone

3c 🎬 **What's the most beautiful place you've ever travelled to?**

c Watch video 3c. Match 1–7 with a–g to make sentences.

1 [g] Ruby remembers
2 ☐ Lauren describes
3 ☐ Jenna talks about
4 ☐ Nora describes
5 ☐ Both Lauren and Nora describe
6 ☐ Nora didn't enjoy
7 ☐ Everybody except Jenna talks about

a very similar beaches.
b sharing the beach.
c walking to the beach.
d the colour of the sea.
e the brilliant pictures she took.
f how the place was like heaven.
g the colours and the heat.

Unit 4: Consciousness

4a ▸ When do the best ideas come to you?

a Watch video 4a. Match 1–7 with a–g to make sentences.

1 [g] Adelaide has good ideas
2 [   ] Adelaide also has good ideas
3 [   ] Alex has a lot of ideas
4 [   ] Caroline has a lot of ideas
5 [   ] Adam has ideas
6 [   ] Two of the speakers have ideas
7 [   ] Three of the speakers have ideas

a late at night.
b while trying to study.
c in the shower.
d in the kitchen.
e when it's not convenient.
f when there's no one else there.
g in the car.

4b ▸ What do you think is meant by a 'sixth sense'?

b Watch video 4b and tick (✓) the correct answers.

1 Adelaide thinks a sixth sense is always felt _____.
  a [   ] as something happens
  b [✓] before something happens
  c [   ] after something has happened

2 Adelaide doesn't have a sixth sense but she knows someone who _____.
  a [   ] might have it
  b [   ] used to have it
  c [   ] does have it

3 Adelaide's sister's boyfriend predicted the incident _____.
  a [   ] in her aunt's car
  b [   ] after being asleep
  c [   ] two hours before

4 Alex feels you cannot _____ a sixth sense.
  a [   ] define
  b [   ] have
  c [   ] acquire

5 _____ have similar definitions of a sixth sense.
  a [   ] Adam and Adelaide
  b [   ] Alex and Adam
  c [   ] Adelaide and Alex

6 Only _____ gives a concrete example of someone's sixth sense.
  a [   ] Adam
  b [   ] Alex
  c [   ] Adelaide

7 _____ they have a sixth sense.
  a [   ] One of the speakers thinks
  b [   ] None of the speakers think
  c [   ] Some of the speakers think

4c ▸ Do you think it's a good idea to trust your instinct?

c Watch video 4c. Underline the correct words to complete the sentences.

1 Adelaide has _changed her mind_ / _kept the same views_ about following her instinct since she was young.
2 Adelaide has _never_ / _sometimes_ accepted job offers against her instinct.
3 Alex believes that his _initial_ / _considered_ thoughts are usually right.
4 Alex feels you _should_ / _shouldn't_ think too much about other people's views.
5 Caroline believes that you can sense danger in _an instinctive_ / _a calculated_ way.
6 All three speakers seem _wary_ / _in favour_ of following their gut reaction.

Unit 5: Fairness

5a ▸ Which kinds of jobs have the best employment conditions?

a Watch video 5a and tick (✓) the correct answers.

1 Anna says that people who work _____ probably have the worst working conditions.
  a [✓] with their hands
  b [   ] in hospitals
  c [   ] in offices

2 Anna probably wouldn't enjoy working _____.
  a [   ] in a hospital
  b [   ] outside in winter
  c [   ] in an office

3 Valentina thinks _____ have difficult working conditions.
  a [   ] office workers
  b [   ] admin staff
  c [   ] soldiers

4 According to Rachel, a _____ would be a good place to work.
  a [   ] local government office
  b [   ] restaurant
  c [   ] local business

5 Matt thinks teachers have _____.
  a [   ] long careers
  b [   ] good pay
  c [   ] job satisfaction

6 At the sandwich shop, Matt's hours were _____.
  a [   ] long
  b [   ] uncertain
  c [   ] horrible

5b 🎥 **How easy is it for people entering your field of work to find a good job?**

b Watch video 5b. <u>Underline</u> the correct words to complete the sentences.

1 Anna says most people start a career in her field <u>*at a low level*</u> / *with some experience*.
2 Anna says that in publishing today, *certain people* / *anybody* can start at a higher level.
3 According to Rachel, the number of applicants for a teaching job often depends on the *salary* / *location*.
4 Rachel thinks *workplace training* / *academic qualifications* can be more useful in finding a job these days.
5 Rachel and Matt both think there are *not enough jobs* / *lots of jobs* for young people these days.
6 Matt thinks schools in England *do enough* / *could do more* to prepare young people for work.

5c 🎥 **If you ran a business, would it be important that your employees enjoyed working there?**

c Watch video 5c. <u>Underline</u> the correct words to complete the sentences.

1 *Anna* / <u>*Rachel*</u> says the boss's door should always be open.
2 *Rachel* / *Stuart* says what you get out of a job should equal what you put in.
3 Stuart and *Anna* / *Rachel* believe that teamwork is important.
4 *Anna* / *Stuart* says staff should only be asked to do tasks they are capable of carrying out.
5 *Rachel* / *Stuart* says it is important that staff know their voices will be heard.
6 *Everyone* / *No one* says satisfied employees are likely to do a better job.

Unit 6: Perspectives

6a 🎥 **Do you take a lot of photos?**

a Watch video 6a. <u>Underline</u> the correct words to complete the sentences.

1 Gill plans to *take more photos* / <u>*organise her photos*</u> when she stops working.
2 Gill and her husband *agree* / *disagree* on the best way to store pictures.
3 David is unlikely to take photos *at home* / *on holiday*.
4 David says he often *shares* / *deletes* the photos on his phone.
5 Rose doesn't always remember *to take* / *to save* photos.
6 Rose would probably *not like* / *like* to print the photos on her computer.
7 Gill and Elizabeth are both married to *keen photographers* / *owners of new cameras*.
8 Elizabeth likes to share her photos *all the time* / *on special occasions*.

6b 🎥 **Are there any professional photos on your walls at home?**

b Watch video 6b. Match the speakers 1–5 with their opinions a–e.

1 [d] Gill
2 [ ] David
3 [ ] Rose
4 [ ] Elizabeth
5 [ ] Emma

a Our family photos are a bit unusual.
b The photos on our walls are there for motivation.
c I like to put up my own photos of friends and family.
d I wanted a photo of the whole family before someone left.
e I haven't had time to put up any photos.

6c 🎥 **What's your favourite picture of yourself or someone in your family?**

c Watch video 6c and tick (✓) the correct answers.

1 Gill thinks photos should _____.
   a [ ] take up wall space
   b [✓] remind us of the past
   c [ ] be of children

2 David likes photos of himself when he has _____.
   a [ ] achieved something
   b [ ] won something
   c [ ] changed

3 David's family _____.
   a [ ] often see each other
   b [ ] meet up on special occasions
   c [ ] live together

4 Rose likes the photo of her grandmother because it _____.
   a [ ] resembles her
   b [ ] brings back memories
   c [ ] is old

5 When they were younger, Elizabeth's sons _____.
   a [ ] were very funny
   b [ ] played together
   c [ ] were not very close

6 Elizabeth likes the photo because it is a reminder of how her boys _____.
   a [ ] used to be alike
   b [ ] used to look
   c [ ] used to act

Unit 7: Connections

7a 📹 **If you had to live in an unfamiliar country where you didn't speak the language, what problems might you encounter?**

a Watch video 7a and tick (✓) the correct answers.

1 Jenny describes a time she found it difficult to

_____.
   a ✓ ask for something
   b ☐ find a supermarket
   c ☐ do the recycling

2 Jenny's attempts to communicate _____.
   a ☐ were unsuccessful
   b ☐ attracted attention
   c ☐ caused confusion

3 Monika doesn't mention the difficulties of _____.
   a ☐ meeting people
   b ☐ using public transport
   c ☐ getting a job

4 Monika suggests _____ might be helpful.
   a ☐ online research
   b ☐ making friends
   c ☐ being a tourist

5 According to Laurence, it would probably be harder to settle in a foreign country if you were _____.
   a ☐ quiet
   b ☐ talkative
   c ☐ confident

6 _____ have personal experience to base their answers on.
   a ☐ Laurence and Monika
   b ☐ Laurence and Jenny
   c ☐ All three

7b 📹 **If you started a job in a small company where everyone knew each other, what problems might you encounter?**

b Watch video 7b. Underline the correct words to complete the sentences.

1 Adelaide thinks it's difficult at first because _groups of friends already exist_ / nobody makes an effort.

2 Adelaide wouldn't recommend _waiting_ / trying to make friends.

3 Laurence feels people might be talking about you _secretly_ / openly at first.

4 Laurence suggests that you should _try different things_ / stick to your own job.

5 All three speakers recommend trying to be _professional_ / sociable.

6 All three speakers talk about the current staff often being _outward_ / inward looking.

7c 📹 **If you met someone online and wanted to get to know them better, what problems might you encounter?**

c Watch video 7c. Match the speakers 1–5 with their opinions a–e.
   1 [e] Adelaide says how easy it is
   2 ☐ Adelaide recommends
   3 ☐ Jenny dislikes
   4 ☐ Monika suggests
   5 ☐ Most of them have concerns about

   a meeting online contacts face to face.
   b having a video conversation before agreeing to meet.
   c informing other people about the time and the place of your meeting.
   d chatting to people online.
   e pretending to be someone else online.

Unit 8: Body and health

8a 📹 **Do you think people will live for longer in the future?**

a Watch video 8a. Underline the correct words to complete the sentences.

1 According to Stuart, our diet these days has _more_ / less nutritional value.

2 Stuart feels people nowadays _know_ / don't know a lot about what is good and bad for our health.

3 Valentina _agrees_ / disagrees with the others.

4 Valentina says that _pollution_ / medicine is an important factor in life expectancy.

5 Anna thinks that many people _will need_ / won't need to change their lifestyle if they want to live longer.

6 Both Anna and Stuart think that we will have more chance of _recovering from_ / getting serious diseases.

8b 📹 **Do you know anyone who's ever followed a diet?**

b Watch video 8b and tick (✓) the correct answers.

1 Some of Stuart's friends diet to improve their

_____.
   a ☐ lifestyle
   b ☐ weight
   c ✓ performance

2 Rachel recommends trying to _____.
   a ☐ eat sensibly
   b ☐ lose weight quickly
   c ☐ cut out certain foods

3 Matt's diet failed because he _____.
   a ☐ didn't know what to cook
   b ☐ didn't like the recipes
   c ☐ didn't have enough determination

4 None of Valentina's friends have _____.
   a ☐ been on diets
   b ☐ lost weight permanently
   c ☐ put on weight

5 Anna's friends have had _____ results from diets.
   a ☐ negative
   b ☐ positive
   c ☐ varied

8c ■◀ What treat would you find most difficult to cut out of your diet?

c Watch video 8c. Match the speakers 1–5 with their opinions a–e.

1 [c] Stuart
2 [ ] Rachel
3 [ ] Anna and Valentina
4 [ ] Valentina
5 [ ] All the speakers

a I love chocolatey treats.
b I would hate to cut out sweet treats.
c I have a weakness for doughnuts.
d I would not want to cut down on desserts.
e I love eating cookies.

Unit 9: Cities

9a ■◀ Has the area you live in changed much in recent years?

a Watch video 9a. Underline the correct words to complete the sentences.

1 Alex feels his home town has more *places to eat* / *independent shops* than it used to.
2 According to Alex, the town has been developed for the benefit of *locals* / *visitors*.
3 Adam *contradicts himself* / *exaggerates* slightly.
4 In Adelaide's home town the population has probably *decreased* / *increased*.
5 Adelaide feels the changes have *improved* / *worsened* the town.
6 Of all the speakers, *Adam* / *Alex* is the most critical of the changes in his home town.

9b ■◀ Are there parts of the town where you live that need redeveloping or regenerating?

b Watch video 9b and tick (✓) the correct answers.

1 Alex argues that improving the outskirts of the town would create _____.
   a [ ] friction
   b [ ] controversy
   c [✓] a positive feeling

2 Alex thinks that his local council needs to give more consideration to its _____.
   a [ ] residents
   b [ ] town centre
   c [ ] tourists

3 Like many tourist destinations, Alex thinks there is _____ felt with regard to visitors in Stratford.
   a [ ] hate
   b [ ] pride
   c [ ] tension

4 Alex thinks that the towns need to make some _____ improvements.
   a [ ] sensible
   b [ ] major
   c [ ] radical

5 Adam makes _____ about how his town looks.
   a [ ] one main point
   b [ ] lots of suggestions
   c [ ] a couple of comments

6 Caroline thinks that every part of _____ needs some improvement.
   a [ ] her town
   b [ ] her region
   c [ ] the UK

7 Caroline is not critical of _____ in Wales.
   a [ ] government spending
   b [ ] public transport
   c [ ] the number of cars on the roads

9c ■◀ If you had a lot of money, what kind of house would you like to live in?

c Watch video 9c. Match 1–5 with a–e to make sentences.

1 [a] Alex probably wouldn't be happy in
2 [ ] Caroline would be happy with
3 [ ] Adam would like
4 [ ] Adelaide would like
5 [ ] Adelaide and Caroline would both like

a a modern house.
b a house with lots of natural light.
c to live somewhere unspoiled.
d a house with plenty of facilities.
e a small house.

Unit 10: Occasions

10a  Do you know of any objects that traditionally bring good luck or ward off evil?

a Watch video 10a. Match 1–5 with a–e to make sentences.

1. ☐ d ☐ Gill mentions
2. ☐ David is uncertain about why
3. ☐ Rose says that in her country
4. ☐ Only Emma mentions
5. ☐ Elizabeth mentions

a jewellery.
b a rabbit's foot is considered lucky.
c a kitchen ingredient.
d a plant and an animal.
e certain creatures are considered lucky.

10b What place do you think superstitions have in today's society?

b Watch video 10b. <u>Underline</u> the correct words to complete the sentences.

1. Gill probably feels that previous generations were *more* / *less* superstitious.
2. According to David, we are less superstitious nowadays because we *know why things happen* / *don't need luck*.
3. Rose feels that views on superstition differ depending on how *wealthy* / *old* you are.
4. Emma would be more likely to *consult an expert* / *wear a charm* if she had a problem.
5. Only Rose considers the question from a *personal* / *global* point of view.
6. David and Emma have quite *different* / *similar* views.

10c Would you describe yourself as a superstitious person?

c Watch video 10c and tick (✓) the correct answers.

1. Gill suggests that luck is something _____.
   a ✓ we can control
   b ☐ we need
   c ☐ we don't understand
2. David thinks that what happens in life occurs because of _____.
   a ☐ luck
   b ☐ your own decisions
   c ☐ a combination of both
3. Rose is _____ her opinion.
   a ☐ certain of
   b ☐ unsure about
   c ☐ hesitant about giving
4. If she had been born somewhere else, Emma _____ have been more superstitious.
   a ☐ would definitely
   b ☐ would definitely not be
   c ☐ might

5. None of the speakers are superstitious _____.
   a ☐ any more
   b ☐ in front of others
   c ☐ in the slightest
6. Both _____ use a similar saying about luck.
   a ☐ Gill and Emma
   b ☐ Rose and Gill
   c ☐ David and Rose

AUDIOSCRIPTS

UNIT 1

▶ 01.01

ROBERT Thank you for coming, Sonia.
SONIA My pleasure. Thank you for the opportunity.
R So how long have you been living in Brighton?
S By December, I'll have been here for two years.
R Have you ever had a job in the hotel industry before?
S Yes, I have. I worked in a hotel in Málaga for eighteen months before I moved here.
R So why did you apply for this particular position?
S As soon as I saw it, I knew it was the right job for me.
R What do you like about it?
S I've always enjoyed working with people and helping them, so this position seems ideal.
R This isn't your first application, is it?
S No, this is the second time I've applied. The first time my English wasn't good enough.
R It sounds good now.
S It has got a lot better. I'd just arrived in Brighton the last time I applied.
R Do you have any questions?
S When will I know if I've got the job?
R We'll have made our decision by the end of next week. Ten days at the most.
S That sounds great. I look forward to hearing from you.

▶ 01.02

1 The team had been training for three months already when the season started.
2 By September, I will have been studying Arabic for three years.
3 This is the fourth time I have tried to learn ballroom dancing.
4 They have been practising this piece on the piano for about three months now.
5 By the time I got to rehearsal, the actors had been working for about an hour.
6 She has been revising for this exam since early this morning.

▶ 01.03

TIM Thanks for helping me with this, Harry. I really appreciate it.
HARRY No problem, Tim.
T This is sort of my first report, and I want to get it right.
H Sure. I still remember my first one.
T You've done loads of them since then, I suppose. How long have you been here?
H Twenty years. Give or take a couple.
T So you've done a lot of reports?
H Quite a few.
T Hundreds, I expect. So who should I copy my report to?
H Whatshisname in Finance and probably that other guy.
T Who?
H Thingy. The tall guy. He's something to do with sales. It'll come back to me. Next question?
T How long should the report be?
H Not too long.
T Quite short then? Good.
H But not too short. Somewhere in the region of three or four pages.
T That's not too hard then. Three to four pages. Plus a cover page. What should I call it?
H *The future of the company.* Or words to that effect.
T Brilliant idea. Final question. Can I buy you lunch?
H Of course you can. What's the budget?
T About a tenner. Will that be enough?
H I suppose it'll have to be. Let's go.

▶ 01.04

1 It's a good career.
2 I prefer the green one.
3 Let's have fruit instead.
4 I never wear a tie.
5 People don't earn much here.
6 Shall we have a break?
7 I don't believe it.
8 I can't bear it.
9 I'm going to the pier.
10 What did you learn?
11 He's a great player.
12 Bread, anyone?

▶ 01.05

ZAC So, Rebecca, what do you do for a living?
REBECCA Well, Zac ... I'm a lexicographer. I write dictionaries.
Z What an unusual job! Lexicographer, did you say? To be honest, I didn't realise that anyone did that these days. I don't mean to be rude, but don't we already have enough dictionaries?
R Well, the thing is, language is constantly changing. For a start, there are loads of new words coming into the language all the time. We could easily add a couple of hundred words to a big dictionary every year.
Z Oh, really? What kind of words?
R 'Zoombombing' is a really good example. We hear it almost every day now, but a few years ago the concept didn't exist.
Z Yes, that's true! But I think I kind of disapprove of words like that. They seem so trivial; they don't deserve a place in the dictionary. Maybe that's because I don't like the idea of Zoombombing. Some people don't just appear uninvited in a group video call; they actually behave in an offensive way.
R You have a point, but we're trained not to think like that. We don't pass judgement on the language; we just record it. And we couldn't disallow Zoombombing just because we don't like people doing it!
Z Well, what about all those ridiculous adaptations – what did I hear? – 'Janxiety' for 'January' and 'anxiety' or 'cli-fi' which combines 'climate' and 'fiction'. Surely you wouldn't put those in?
R It depends. A lot of words do prove to be rather ephemeral, and we have to take them back out of the dictionary in the next edition. That's particularly true of anything involving technology, where ongoing change means that some words barely have time to be invented before they're on their way out again – just like the things they describe!
Z OK, I get it that technology produces a lot of new words, but what else?
R Fashion is one.
Z Because it changes all the time?
R That's right. And it seems to produce an endless stream of what we call portmanteau words. That's where two words are stuck together to make one. Things like 'skort': a cross between a skirt and shorts; or 'jeggings': leggings that look like jeans.
Z Oh, yes! My colleague was talking yesterday about the delicious 'froyo' she'd had at lunchtime. It turned out simply to be a frozen yoghurt. That must be the same phenomenon!
R Exactly. And in fact, food is another fertile area for us lexicographers. We're always finding new things to eat.
Z Well, that may be true, but I definitely don't want to see froyo in the dictionary!

UNIT 2

▶ 02.01

I recently experienced one of the most silent nights of my life. I was visiting friends in Riyadh and they suggested going out to the desert. We left the city at dusk and the further we went, the darker it got. After about two hours, we arrived at the camp and pitched our tent. It was considerably colder than I had expected, but the view was stunning. All I could hear was my own breathing as I looked at the most amazing sky. The stars were much clearer and more numerous than I had ever experienced. That night, I definitely felt significantly more aware of the size of the universe.

▶ 02.02

A So, tell me all. How was the big meeting?
B It was a bit more relaxed than I'd expected.
A So did you manage to fit in with all those important people?
B I guess so. I hope I came across well – there were a number of people I could relate to.
A How was the 'Big Boss'?
B He was OK. When I first got there, he bombarded me with questions about our current project. Overall, I think I did quite well, actually. Mind you, my thoughts on the manager nearly slipped out.
A I hope you held yourself back.
B Of course I did. Some of the discussions brought out the worst in some of the participants. One man went on and on about the budget. It was as if he was the only one affected. Anyway, the whole thing was fine. It was a great day and I learned lots.
A Well done! You obviously handled the whole thing very professionally.

▶ 02.03

1 It was a bit more relaxed than I'd expected.
2 So did you manage to fit in with all those important people?
3 Overall, I think I did quite well, actually.
4 One man went on and on about the budget.
5 It was a great day and I learned lots.

▶ 02.04

MARCO What's the problem, Luisa?
LUISA Nothing major. Well, actually ... Don't you dare tell anyone, but I'm thinking of leaving.
M You? Quitting? Why?
L My job is quite dull and the manager doesn't seem to realise I'm bored.
M Have you told him?
L Indirectly. I've dropped lots of hints.
M Yes, but there's a lot to be said for being upfront. You need to tell him directly.
L He won't listen.
M It might even be in your interests to go above him and talk to his manager. It's high time you sorted this problem out.
L I don't think I could do that, Marco. That's not really my style. I just need a new challenge and I don't think I'm going to get it here and that's that.
M Don't get so defensive about it. Why don't you speak to HR?
L There's no point.
M I disagree. You might want to try this. Have you thought about the possibility of asking for a secondment or even a sabbatical?
L A sabbatical? That's not a bad idea. OK, I'll give it some thought.

1 **A** Why don't you come with me?
   B I am sure you'll be fine on your own.
2 **A** There's a lot to be said for cycling to work.
   B I agree. Cheaper and healthier.
3 **A** You might want to read this.
   B Really? What's it about?
4 **A** It's about time you went home.
   B I will as soon as I've finished this.
5 **A** You might as well cancel the meeting.
   B Why? How many can't come?

1 **A** Did the manager email the supplier last week?
   B No, she telephoned them last week.
2 **A** Did the manager email the supplier last week?
   B No, she emailed them last month.
3 **A** Did all the participants speak English during the meeting?
   B No, everyone spoke German during the meeting.
4 **A** Did all the participants speak English during the meeting?
   B No, but the presenters spoke English.
5 **A** Will you be going to Italy on holiday again this year?
   B No, but I'll be going there for work.
6 **A** Will you be going to Italy on holiday again this year?
   B No, I think we'll be going to Greece.
7 **A** Are you flying to the meeting in Paris next week?
   B No, I think I'll be driving there.
8 **A** So you are doing a presentation in Berlin?
   B No, I'm doing a workshop in Berlin.

CARLA Rakesh! Rakesh, I haven't seen you for ages! How are you doing?
RAKESH Oh hi, Carla. Not that great, actually.
C Oh? What's up, if you don't mind me asking?
R Well, this is probably going to sound really stupid to you, but I seem to have lost my sense of smell. And I know it sounds really trivial, but it's driving me crazy. For one thing, I can't really taste things any more, and you know how I love my food!
C I thought you said you'd lost your sense of smell, not taste.
R Yeah, but apparently about 80% of the taste of food comes from the smell. Your taste buds can only detect a few flavours. My girlfriend's getting fed up with me complaining about it, but she doesn't understand. Eating's just a function for me now, and it should be one of life's great pleasures!
C No, I totally get it. My uncle had the same thing after he had a stroke. We all thought he'd recovered apart from having a slight limp, but he seemed to cut himself off from the rest of the family and when Mum spoke to him, he said that was the reason. He still finds it really frustrating, not being able to experience things everyone else can, like the smell of flowers or food cooking on the barbecue.
R Yeah, you just take all these things for granted before it happens to you.
C And it can be dangerous, too. I hope you've checked all your smoke alarms!
R Yes, my doctor gave me a brochure about all the precautions I need to take, like installing a gas detector and remembering to look at all the use-by dates on food, because I have no other way of knowing if it's gone off.
C What a pain! So what caused it? You haven't had a head injury, have you?
R Don't worry, it isn't anything *that* serious. My doctor isn't sure, but I'm due to see a specialist at the hospital next week and hopefully he'll be able to diagnose the underlying cause. Apparently, there are two basic possibilities: either something is stopping the odours from reaching the top of my nose, or something is interfering with the nerve signals between the brain and the nose.
C Well, I hope he gets to the bottom of it for you.
R Thanks. And one good thing to come out of it is that I'm going to start eating more healthily and lose a few kilos. I know it hasn't caused this problem, but if I can't even enjoy all the fried food, it's probably in my interests to stop eating it!
C That's great. Good luck with that!

UNIT 3

A How would you describe your early life?
B Well, life was pretty tough. There was a lot of financial hardship.
A Where were you brought up?
B In a rather deprived area with poor housing and not many amenities.
A Were you very poor?
B No, not really. We weren't exactly impoverished. We were never rich but never destitute either. We had just enough money to live on and were careful to live within our means.
A Now that you've become rich and have a large disposable income, how has your life changed?
B Well, obviously I don't have to worry about making ends meet. We live in a nice house in an affluent area.
A And are you happier?
B A good question. I would say my life is pretty comfortable now, but prosperity doesn't always necessarily bring you happiness.

neighbouring
charity
poverty
destitute
relatives
enrolment
everyone
volunteer
requirement
improvement
nutritious

In late 2008, Oliver Broom was working in London. Having graduated a few years before, he was earning a good salary and to all intents and purposes had a bright future, but Oli had other things on his mind. A good friend had been seriously injured swimming on holiday some time before and this had made him question what he was doing with his life. On top of that, he had just split up with his girlfriend and he realised that if he was going to do something different with his life, then the time was ripe.

One of his hobbies was cricket – playing it and watching it – and he suddenly had the craziest of ideas and decided he would cycle to Australia in time to see England play their next match against Australia, which was set to take place two years hence. He worked out a possible route which would take him through over twenty countries, ending with a sea-crossing from Indonesia to North Australia, before the final leg from Darwin to Brisbane, which was going to be another 5,000 kilometres.

He said he would spend the first few months in Europe pedalling through France and Germany down to the Danube, which he planned to follow as far as possible. 'It will be getting cold by then, so I'll pedal on towards Istanbul and the gateway to Asia,' he predicted as he set off in October 2009.

Things didn't quite work out as planned and, by the time he arrived in Thailand, he had already had to make major changes to his schedule due to the weather, war and various other factors. No sooner had he arrived in Thailand than he was suddenly struck down with dengue fever and was hospitalised, leaving him unsure if he would be able to carry on or not. Luckily, he managed to recover and caught his ship to Australia on time and completed the journey across the outback to Brisbane. With remarkable timing, Oli cycled into Brisbane the very day the cricket match was to start.

Your brother's got amazing hair!
I've got four exams tomorrow.
That's the biggest egg I've ever seen!
I can't find my keys!
What a great dinner – it looks delicious.
Look at his car – it's so dirty.
I can't ask him to help me again – he's done enough already.
My husband's great in a crisis. He always knows what to do.
That's the biggest fish I've ever seen!
My husband's a great cook.

ALEX Hi, Dario. So what's this news you wanted to tell me?
DARIO Well, it really is quite exciting. Basically, I have decided not to start work just yet.
A Not work? But I thought you had a job offer.
D I have, but, you know, we've only just graduated and I've been studying, taking exams, revising and so on for years. In a nutshell, I fancy doing something different and going somewhere new.
A In other words, you're going travelling again.
D But not just for pleasure. I did some reading, talked to some people, did some desk research, sent off some emails and, to cut a long story short, I'm off to Uganda.
A Wow! Africa. To do what?
D Well, I wanted to do something meaningful, you know, help others. Give something back.
A Not like people like me then!
D No, what I meant was that for me it's important to test myself a bit. Get out of the comfort zone. So I'm going to help build a primary school.
A A school? That will be amazing! You out in the African heat and me at my hot desk at the bank. That just about sums it up. So when are you off?
D In two weeks. Can't wait. So much to do.
A Can I just say … How shall I put this? I'm very proud.

1 just graduated
2 difficult to explain
3 desk research
4 somewhere new
5 something meaningful
6 the young should support
7 not just for pleasure
8 vegetables probably

GEMMA We've been learning about explorers at school and I really want to be one!
MUM Really? I must say, all that hacking through dense jungle and trekking across arid deserts never appealed to me.
G Oh, Mum, where's your sense of adventure? These people have a place in history!
M Like Marco Polo and Christopher Columbus, you mean?
G Well, yeah, but more modern people too. And plenty of women. There were some fantastic ones around the end of the nineteenth, beginning of the twentieth century; I wish I'd been born then, when travelling was still so exciting and romantic! Like Gertrude Bell, for instance. She was a real intellectual. She had pots of money, and she travelled around and she learned how to speak Arabic and Persian and goodness knows what else. She wasn't just a tourist, though. She ended up having an immense amount of power and playing a major role in establishing Iraq – the modern state, that is.
M I feel exhausted just thinking about it.
G Oh, Mum! Well, what about Amelia Earhart? She was such a pioneer – the first female aviator to fly solo over the Atlantic.
M But she died really young, didn't she? Went missing in the Pacific if I remember correctly. It's all very well being adventurous, but if you die in the process …
G But people still remember her now; that counts for something, doesn't it? And not only did she break all those records herself, but she also inspired so many other women and made them believe they could do things just like men.

M Yes, well, you can do what you like if you have plenty of money, but you're going to have to live within your means.

G I know that, but there are plenty of examples of people whose job gives them adventure. Like, have you heard of Martha Gellhorn? She actually started off travelling around America interviewing people made destitute by the Great Depression, but she ended up being one of the greatest war correspondents of the twentieth century, reporting on almost every major conflict in the sixty years she was working.

M But is there actually anywhere left to explore these days?

G Yes, lots of places, obviously!

M What do you mean?

G Space, of course! Valentina Tereshkova was the first woman in space, but there are still plenty of challenges, and ones we're probably going to have to face if we carry on trashing the planet the way we're doing now. Perhaps I'll be one of the first people to go to Mars. That would be so cool. There's only one problem with that, though.

M What's that?

G Well, you can get there, but currently there's no way of coming home again.

M Oh, Gemma!

UNIT 4

▶ **04.01**

A How do you decide to buy something?

B Well, it depends on what it is.

A What do you mean?

B If it's a house, for instance, I'd weigh up the advantages and disadvantages first and then think it over for a while.

A So you tend to think logically?

B Yes, I suppose I'm a rational thinker. How about you?

A Well, I'd probably go with my gut instinct in that situation.

B So you'd buy a house on impulse, without thinking?

A Not necessarily, but I'd know subconsciously that it was the right thing to do. Don't you ever make a spontaneous decision?

B Yes, of course. I wouldn't think twice about buying a new pair of shoes! I love to keep up with fashion!

▶ **04.02**

1 I remember when I was very young.
2 We always went on holiday to Italy.
3 In the evening, we would walk by the lake.
4 My brothers put me in a rowing boat.
5 I still have my photo album to refresh my memory.

▶ **04.03**

A What did you think of the presentation?

B No offence intended, but I found it dull.

A I think I see where you're coming from, but I beg to differ.

B So you found it interesting?

A Well, not exactly interesting, but dull is a little harsh.

B With all due respect, it's much better to be frank. It was boring.

A OK, I take your point. It wasn't that interesting, but we need to be more supportive.

B I disagree. In fact, if you don't mind me saying so, he needs to be told.

A I'll leave that to you then. You're his manager!

▶ **04.04**

1 I have eight brothers.
2 When I was a child, I was only allowed to eat sweets once a week.
3 My mother dyed the sheets blue.
4 I had to brake very late to avoid an accident.
5 I eat out at least three times a week.
6 They want to place the new conference table here.
7 The strong winds blew the parasols over.
8 This coat was half price in the sale.

▶ **04.05**

LEILA A really embarrassing thing happened to me last week, Hannah. I was in this museum in York, and they had all these rooms decorated in the styles of different decades. We came to this one from the 1980s and I just burst into tears because it was my grandmother's living room, right there in the museum!

HANNAH What, her actual furniture and stuff?

L No, I just mean that it was so similar. Although, to be honest, I only have a pretty vague memory of her living room; she died when I was twelve. Whether it was the wallpaper or the furniture, I'm not sure, but there was something there that triggered these really strong memories. I felt like I could almost smell it; her house always had a very distinctive smell of perfume and baking bread; and I could remember the taste of this particular kind of cake she used to get delivered when we came to visit.

H That's really moving, Leila. It's so weird how that kind of thing can happen, isn't it? I get it with music sometimes. Some song you hear on the radio brings back vivid memories of a time in your past.

L Yeah, I saw a documentary on TV about using music with people who have memory problems, and they were talking about how we have different kinds of memory.

H Yes, I saw that too – fascinating!

L I think they said there's 'explicit' memory, where we're actually trying to remember things like information for an exam, and then there's 'implicit' memory, which is all the stuff we don't make a conscious effort to remember. Didn't the documentary say that those memories get stored in different parts of the brain, and the part that stores implicit memories is a lot more robust? So even for someone who has almost completely lost touch with reality, music can still re-awaken distant memories.

H That's right! That old man with Alzheimer's disease who'd been totally uncommunicative for months started singing and dancing, didn't he?

L Yes, it was so moving! But I've never really understood why silly little pop songs can have such a powerful effect. I can't believe some of the terrible songs that can bring a tear to my eye!

H Well, even if the songs themselves are totally worthless, they still have that association with memories that we really treasure. For me, they're mostly connected to when I was younger; things like travelling in South America or being at university. I did listen to classical music then, too, but it's just a bit too abstract somehow to have the same effect.

L Yes, and pop music is more of a shared experience. In fact, do you remember how that documentary showed them using particular songs to try to connect the patients with their visitors? It made me think about what song I'd use to remember my husband.

H And did you decide?

L Yes, it would have to be John Legend's *All of Me*. We played that at our wedding.

UNIT 5

▶ **05.01**

comparison
mission
occasion
Asian
person
Russian
passion
imprisonment
cousin
dismiss
pressure
collision

▶ **05.02**

1 Could you give me your contact details?
2 We couldn't find any record of a meeting on that date.
3 We export about 45% of our production.
4 We are starting the research in Liberia next month.
5 We need to increase the number of international contracts we get.
6 We produce most of our own vegetables.

▶ **05.03**

1 **A** I thought I remembered you saying you played squash.
  B That's right. Do you?
2 **C** Have you ever been diving?
  D Yes, I have. What stands out in my mind is seeing a huge turtle.
3 **A** No doubt you've already researched the best restaurants in the neighbourhood.
  B Of course! What else was I going to do while I was hungry on the train?
4 **C** Judging from your appearance, I'd hazard a guess at 30.
  D Very good! I turn 31 next month.
5 **A** I was under the impression you spoke Thai.
  B No, I don't, although I worked in Pattaya for a couple of months.
6 **C** Presumably you have a degree.
  D Well, actually, I went to university but left after two years.

▶ **05.04**

1 I bet you it'll rain tomorrow just because it's the weekend.
2 I was under the impression it was open on Mondays.
3 I'd hazard a guess you work in marketing of some sort.
4 I'm guessing you're a sports fan.
5 I'm sure I remember my father telling me that joke.
6 No doubt you'll be surprised but I am actually Canadian.
7 Suppose you'd been born in Germany, how different would your life be?
8 What stands out for me about the eighties is the music.
9 Without a shadow of a doubt, the value of gold will continue to rise.

▶ **05.05**

1 He's not just any footballer … he's the world's best footballer.
2 Some countries simply copy, … while other countries create.
3 It's not just the money … it's the time and the money.
4 I don't know any jokes … I don't know any good jokes anyway.
5 The lesson wasn't just difficult … it was difficult and boring.

▶ **05.06**

ADRIANA Hi, I'm Adriana. The best thing about my job is that no two days are the same. One day I might be called upon to give evidence at a trial, and the next be out and about in the city, investigating a crime. This job's definitely not for the fainthearted. Every call we get can lead us into a potentially dangerous situation. I do have colleagues who have suffered assaults, a couple of whom have been quite seriously injured, but we're well trained, and the knowledge that we're protecting the public makes that risk worth taking. I work a shift system, about 40 hours a week, but of course I can't just drop everything and go home if I'm in the middle of an investigation, so juggling my job with my responsibilities as a parent can be interesting, to say the least! I have to say, though, that the thing that really gets me down is the mountains of paperwork. It's important to keep records, but I think things have got out of hand in the public sector these days.

BEN Hi, I'm Ben. I work as an environmental engineer for an organisation called Engineers Without Borders. I've worked in the energy sector for most of my adult life, but I've only worked for this organisation for the last couple of years. My job involves developing and building solutions to environmental problems all over the world. With this organisation, we're required to work in developing countries and often in some harsh conditions. It's tough and sometimes dangerous work; for example, countries that don't have access to clean drinking water often have other problems, too. But the hardest part of all is being away from my family for weeks at a time. It pays well, though, and it's very satisfying to know that I'm helping these countries develop environmentally friendly solutions so their people can live longer and healthier lives.

MARTINA   Hi, I'm Martina. Do you buy fresh fruit and vegetables a lot in your local supermarket? Do you ever wonder where it comes from? That's where I come in. I've been employed over the summer on a farm to help with the harvest. I pick fruit, but I also do everything from stacking fruit to lifting it, selecting it and throwing it away!
The agency that found me the job called it employment; I call it exploitation! I knew that wages in the agricultural sector were low, but we're paid the minimum wage, and then out of that we're expected to pay for the horrible little rooms they call our accommodation. It's backbreaking work, and my boss is extremely strict, and sometimes rude and unpleasant. But the thing that annoys me most of all is that they only give us work when they want to, and we never get enough hours. I wanted to save up for studying at university, but it's almost impossible!

UNIT 6

▶ 06.01

A   What did you think of the exhibition?
B   She's a brilliant photographer. The pictures are so evocative of the 1950s.
A   They really are. Her subjects come across as very natural; there is nothing elaborate about the shots.
B   I agree, and there's such variety. Some, such as the shots of the homeless people, are quite gritty, but then you get others that are really playful and make you smile.
A   That's true. She definitely can't be accused of being repetitive.
B   It's amazing to think these photos were nearly lost forever. Some of her photos, like the ones of the Statue of Liberty, are very powerful, particularly as that is itself an iconic image. But the way it's composed with the people in the foreground makes it very meaningful.

▶ 06.02

1   She was so disillusioned.
2   She was so disillusioned.
3   I was absolutely petrified.
4   I was absolutely petrified.
5   I felt extremely frustrated.
6   I felt extremely frustrated.
7   They were very jealous.
8   They were very jealous.
9   I'm really ashamed.
10 I'm really ashamed.

▶ 06.03

1   Thanks very much for your warm welcome. My focus today is regional development, with a particular emphasis on Latin America.
2   One thing is clear: we really need to have a larger presence in this region if we wish to increase our market share.
3   First and foremost, I would like to give you some statistics about the country, which will put things into perspective.
4   It's perfectly obvious that, with a market this size, we need good distribution, and that is one of the areas I would like to talk you through.
5   Moving on from distribution, let's now turn to finance and look at the numbers.
6   This table shows the population by age and area, and I would like to take you through it in some detail.
7   So in conclusion, this is the region I feel we should concentrate on – more specifically, these two cities.
8   So to recap what I've been saying, this is a great opportunity and I would like to offer my full support for this initiative.
9   If you'd like me to elaborate on anything, please let me know.

▶ 06.04

1   Generally speaking, the average working week is 42 hours.
2   Here you get four weeks' paid holiday a year as a rule.

3   As a rule, I'm the last to leave the office.
4   In fact, in some countries you don't get any holiday during your first six months.
5   I think I prefer the European system on the whole.
6   I didn't really enjoy working for that firm, truth be told.
7   Normally, I have two large meals a day.
8   Actually, it's a public holiday here tomorrow.

▶ 06.05

LEWIS   I've noticed that you've been getting a lot of your photos in the papers recently, Martha. You must be doing really well.

MARTHA   I don't know, Lewis. The money's nice of course, but to be honest, I'm getting a bit disillusioned with the whole thing. We're being asked to poke our noses into people's private lives so much, and I'm not sure I want to do that any more.

L   Really? I've always felt a bit jealous of your job; flying off to fabulous places to photograph celebrities doing their shopping, while I get commissioned to take gritty shots of refugee camps or earthquake zones.

M   But at least your work is meaningful, Lewis. It's vital that people know what's going on in the world, and you're a witness to that. My stuff is just so superficial; who cares what designer handbag this or that supermodel is carrying? Not me, that's for sure. And I've been thinking about it all more and more since I had my daughter; all this obsession with fashion and physical appearance, it's not healthy, and I feel ashamed to be contributing to it.

L   I do see what you mean, but I wouldn't recommend my job to you. I was in Pakistan last month when they had that earthquake, and I was absolutely terrified. Seeing all the horror and destruction affected me really badly. I couldn't sleep for days.

M   I'm not surprised. It must have been incredibly traumatic. That's why I admire photographers like you. The most danger I have to face is when some celebrity catches me snooping round their house and sets the dogs on me! But seriously, I'm not saying I'd rather do your job. I don't have the courage, and it wouldn't really be fair on my daughter either. No, I've been thinking about changing careers completely, actually.

L   Oh? Do you have something in mind?

M   Well, I was moaning to my husband about how rubbish it is to be making a living out of invading other people's privacy and he said, 'Well, what's the thing you like doing most?' And when I thought about it, it was obvious: acting. I've been doing amateur stuff for years, so I'm thinking about trying to get into a proper drama school. I know it's insecure, but I could always do a bit of wedding photography on the side.

L   I think it sounds incredibly exciting.

M   The thing is, I'm thirty now and, if I don't do it soon, I never will. It's easy to keep finding excuses not to do things, isn't it? But as you say, I'm selling lots of photographs at the moment, so I'll be reasonably financially secure for a while.

L   In that case, I think you should definitely go for it. Wow, you're making me think. Perhaps it's time for a change for me, too.

M   Well, same question then: what do you like doing most?

L   Um, watching Manchester United play football, probably. I don't think I can make a career out of that, though!

UNIT 7

▶ 07.01

A   Hi, Lewis. Good to see you again. What are you doing here? I thought you worked in the Madrid office.
B   I do, but I'm here for an interview for account executive.
A   Wow. You should have told me. We could have met up last night.

B   I had dinner with Rob. I couldn't have prepared for the interview without his help.
A   So, what are you going to tell them?
B   Well … it's likely that the new system will be a great improvement. We seem to be having difficulties getting paid, so the new process may well improve things.
A   What do you think your chances are?
B   Pretty good, I think. They almost certainly won't give it to an external candidate, and there's a reasonable chance I am the only applicant!
A   Well, good luck! If you're successful, we're bound to be seeing more of each other.

▶ 07.02

1   The person I'd most like to thank is Charles.
2   The reason I'm here is to help you.
3   The one thing I cannot do is cook.
4   What went wrong was I lost my ticket and got fined.
5   The main reason I cycle to work is to save money.
6   The only thing I ask is that you try your best.
7   What will happen is someone will be waiting with your name on a sign.
8   What they proposed was impossible to deliver.

▶ 07.03

A   So what do people think of this plan for a weekend hike? Will it improve staff morale?
B   Who came up with that terrible idea?
A   I did, along with some of the other managers.
B   Sorry, maybe I was out of order, but do you really think a 20-kilometre walk in the hills will improve the atmosphere? I've had it up to here with some of the recent suggestions.
A   Excuse me?
B   I apologise, but when will you understand that the staff want higher wages? That's all. Any other ideas dreamed up by you and your colleagues are just a waste of time.
C   Steady on, John.
B   Sorry, that wasn't very tactful of me. I had no right to take it out on you, but the staff are unhappy.
A   We know they are, but we don't need people like you interfering.
B   So making constructive suggestions is interfering, is it?
A   That was inexcusable of me. But you need to understand that simply paying people more would be a senseless waste of money.
C   That's going a bit far, don't you think?
A   Sorry. I don't know what came over me.
B   I was only trying to help.
A   Yes. I guess I overreacted. Again, I apologise. Now, where were we?

▶ 07.04

1   route
2   although
3   brought
4   dough
5   tough
6   bough
7   would
8   four
9   announce
10 thought
11 through
12 conscious
13 south
14 could
15 southern
16 cough

▶ 07.05

INGRID   Carlo, have you heard that they're thinking of using robots to help elderly people look after themselves? I think it's absolutely terrible. Loneliness is already a huge problem for lots of them and this won't help at all. It's obvious that robots can never replace the intimacy of real human contact.

CARLO   Well, from what I heard about it, they're not intended to replace human carers, but just to give people a bit more back-up when they need it. Things like reminding them when to take their medication or prompting them to eat or drink if they haven't for a while.

I Well, I don't know. I think it's heartbreaking to think of some lonely person being given instructions by a machine. A cup of tea and a hug would do them a lot more good.

C I know what you're saying, Ingrid, but services are already stretched to the limit. The point is, if robots could ease that pressure even by a small amount, it would free up more resources for just the kind of thing you're talking about.

I Hah! I admire your optimism, but I'm afraid I'm more cynical than you. I think that the government will just go for the quickest and easiest option every time. If they can replace expensive, unreliable humans with machines, they will! After all, robots don't go off sick or ask for a pay rise, do they? We could easily be facing a situation where there's even less personal care in the future.

C But a lot of the people who'd be using these robots don't actually live alone. And it would be less of a strain on the people they do live with if a robot could help them with some of the things they need to do. Imagine never being able to go out in case your husband or wife forgets to take their tablets. It'd be impossible to lead a normal life!

I I suppose so. But aren't they quite complicated to use? How do we know that the people they're meant to help will actually understand how to work them?

C Well, apparently there have been trials in the Netherlands, and they worked quite well. They've got touchscreens that're very simple to use. What's crucial is to programme them and train them appropriately, for example, to recognise the user's voice. And nobody's being forced to use every facility a robot can offer – just the ones that are relevant to them.

I I still think it's a poor substitute for proper, personal care. We're hard-wired to need company, and we don't do well without it.

C Well, there's some evidence that robots can actually help to reduce social exclusion by encouraging and reminding users to keep in contact with their friends and families.

I I'm not convinced ... although I guess I might like a robot who could do my cooking and ironing for me.

C Sadly, I don't think they'll be doing that any time soon!

UNIT 8

▶ 08.01

1 I didn't sleep a wink last night!
2 I usually sleep like a log.
3 I'm often fast asleep by 11.
4 I'm going to have a nap later.
5 I just lie there, wide awake.
6 Make sure you don't oversleep.

▶ 08.02

Three-step plan to a better life.
Are you showing your age? Do you have saggy skin, fine lines and wrinkles?
Are you prone to dry skin? Is your hair thinning and greying?
Adopt our plan to prevent those visible signs of ageing.
Step 1. Moisturise and have weekly facials to tighten and plump the skin.
Step 2. Eat a varied and balanced diet to lose weight and get yourself a glowing complexion.
Step 3. Help poor circulation and prevent heart trouble by doing regular cardiovascular exercise.

▶ 08.03

1 Take your eggs, three will do, and break them in a bowl.
2 Take a whisk, or a fork, and beat them.
3 Add some salt and pepper, just a little, and stir.
4 Take some hard cheese, around 30 grams, and grate it.
5 Melt some butter, about 10 grams, in a frying pan.
6 Pour the mix – the eggs – into the pan and cook for a minute or two.
7 Add the cheese and wait, probably a minute, until it melts.
8 Serve immediately.

▶ 08.04

A Hello?
B Hi, I'm phoning about the car you're advertising on the website.
A Oh, great. Are you interested in buying it then?
B Yes, although it depends a bit on what we can do about the price.
A Well, it says 3,200 on the website, but I'd be prepared to accept 3,000.
B I'm afraid I can't go higher than 2,500.
A It's worth much more than that. You won't find a car like it cheaper anywhere else.
B OK, 2,800, but that's as high as I can go.
A Could you see your way to increasing that a little?
B Sorry, that's my final offer.
A I was kind of hoping for 2,900.
B Unfortunately, I'm buying the car for a client and I'm not authorised to go any higher.
A OK. Are you free on Monday to come over and do the paperwork?
B Yes, that's fine.

▶ 08.05

1 I was thinking about a dessert.
2 I was thinking about a dessert.
3 You sound French to me.
4 You sound French to me.
5 I'm not sure if you were there last week.
6 I'm not sure if you were there last week.
7 I was considering a takeaway tonight.
8 I was considering a takeaway tonight.
9 I'm doing some work for, you know, Oxfam.
10 I'm doing some work for, you know, Oxfam.
11 We could go out at, say, ten.
12 We could go out at, say, ten.

▶ 08.06

MARIA Oh, hello, Ralf. I haven't seen you in a while. I hear you're going to be 70 next month. Are you planning a big celebration?

RALF You must be joking, Maria. What is there to celebrate? Wrinkles? Arthritis? False teeth?

M Oh, come on, Ralf, you're not doing that badly! If I were you, I'd be celebrating the fact that I'd made it this far, that I had a lovely, happy family, that I had plenty of leisure time, and –

R Oh, don't start telling me to count my blessings! I've had enough of that from my wife. I just feel that old people are discriminated against all the time in our society. There's so much ageism; people seem to think that just because your hair's thinning that your brain cells are thinning, too. Nobody takes you seriously any more, and I'm fed up with people talking to me as if I were a child.

M Well, it's no use moaning about it. We need to show them that we still have a lot to contribute to society. Look at all the volunteering we do, for a start!

R Yes, of course we do, but are we appreciated? I don't think so. Exploited more like! Think about all the childcare we provide; my son and his wife both have to work, so we do a lot with the grandchildren. We have three of them to stay for two nights a week, and they're quite a handful, I can tell you! Suppose we all said no, enough, we've raised our own children and now we want to relax; what would happen then? The country would grind to a halt.

M You're right about that. But surely your son is grateful for your help?

R Yes, to be fair I think he is, but I don't think that society as a whole values that sort of thing. It's all about youth and status these days; once you're over 60, you're on the rubbish heap.

M I think you're exaggerating wildly, but it's true that we're expected to keep trying to look young, as if it's somehow wrong to show your age. My friend Kathy, who's 64, was telling me the other day that she's considering plastic surgery to get rid of the saggy skin round her neck. I couldn't believe my ears! Even if I had the money, I wouldn't spend it on that. I'd rather go on a cruise or something.

R I totally agree, but I can see why some people can't bear the idea of getting older, because it has such negative connotations: forgetful and confused, set in our ways, don't know how to use the Internet, won't stop talking about the old days; you know the sort of thing.

M I do know, Ralf, but if you don't mind me saying so, I think you're in danger of falling into a stereotype yourself.

R Oh? Which one?

M Grumpy old man!

UNIT 9

▶ 09.01

In the 1980s, the waterfront in Wellington, New Zealand's capital, had become an industrial wasteland right in the centre of the city. As shipping had modernised, a new container port had been built, leaving the old dockland area in need of regeneration.

Wellington is no stranger to redesigning itself. In fact, in the 100 years prior to this project, the city had carried out three different projects to restore its famous waterfront. But this last time, it was vital that the renovated waterfront combined areas for work, recreation, tourism and events. It was also key to the success of the project that the area was re-established as a central hub for the city. The city had a number of different ideas on how they might redevelop the area, and officials began with a design competition to encourage original and innovative thinking.

The whole project took around 20 years and it completely rejuvenated the city. Even nature has had an opportunity to shine. Ducks and other wildlife have found new habitats in the wetland recreated on Wellington's waterfront, known as Waitangi Park. It's become New Zealand's largest new urban park in the last 100 years.

The waterfront now hums with street theatre, music and performance spaces. Restaurants and bars are full of a mix of professionals and tourists, delighted to be in a city that has regained its position as one of the best urban tourism destinations in the world, but hasn't forgotten its connection with nature. Welcome back to Windy Wellington.

▶ 09.02

cabin
apartment
penthouse
skyscraper
mansion
tasteless
nondescript
graceful
innovative
imposing
stunning
power

▶ 09.03

TONY Is that you, Sophie?
SOPHIE Yes, it is. How can I help?
T This is Tony Allen from GK Partners. I'm calling to express my utter disbelief.
S What seems to be the problem, Tony?
T How can I put this? I understand you are in talks with our main competitor.
S Well, I'm not, but a colleague is.
T I'm absolutely lost for words.
S What can I say? I take full responsibility, but you mustn't overreact.
T This is beyond belief. I thought we had an agreement.
S Let's not jump to any conclusions. We are simply talking to them – that is all.
T But you have no right to work with both of us. What on earth happened to our confidentiality agreement?
S There's no reason to raise your voice. I'm sure we can find a solution.
T You'd better, otherwise there will be consequences.
S I understand where you're coming from. I will investigate and get straight back to you.

1 abseil
2 baguette
3 cello
4 mosquito

▶ 09.05

BEN Have you been down to the river recently, Eva? They've revamped the whole area. It looks really cool now.

EVA Oh yes, they've converted all those old warehouses, haven't they? I don't know, Ben, I guess it looks better, but it just feels to me as though they're cramming apartment blocks into every spare inch of the city these days.

B We need the housing, though.

E Yes, but whether that's the kind of housing we need is another question. Where are the family homes for people like us, with kids? It's mostly studio flats in those blocks, for people who work in London. They don't really live there, they just sleep there.

B They need to sleep somewhere, Eva!

E I know they do, but it's a matter of degree. That sort of accommodation just isn't conducive to a stable population, where people get to know their neighbours and become integrated in the community. In my opinion, there should be more mixed housing so that we can all live together – single people, families, older people – everyone. But that's not so lucrative for the developers, is it? They want to squeeze every last penny of profit out of their land.

B Sure, but doesn't the council have some responsibility, too? What on earth happened to urban planning?

E That's true, but the councils actually have less power than you might imagine. They can't turn down planning applications just because they don't like them; they have to have very strong legal reasons. They can't fight them as often as they'd like to because going to court is so expensive, and of course it's taxpayers' money they're spending when they do.

B So do you think it's time to stop building more homes here?

E No, I've got no objection to the building itself, but if I was in charge, I'd be doing it on some of those horrible fields around the outskirts of the city.

B What, on the green belt? I think that's a terrible idea! The green belt's really important to the quality of the air, and it would be awful to build over lovely fields and forests.

E Have you seen the green belt here? A lot of it's just muddy wasteland. But if you don't want to build on it, how about knocking down some of those enormous houses right next to it? Those people really make me mad; they'll protest till they're blue in the face if someone wants to build a house that will spoil their view, but you could fit twenty little houses like mine on the land their mansions take up.

B Wow, Eva, you're so passionate about this! You should stand for the council!

E No, we've got another plan, actually.

B What's that?

E We've found this run-down old cottage in a little village near the coast. We're thinking of renovating it and moving there with the kids.

B That's exciting!

E Yes, it is. And you're welcome to come and visit, any time you get fed up with this crowded old city!

UNIT 10

▶ 10.01

I gave a presentation in Turkey last month and everything that could possibly go wrong went wrong. I should never have agreed to do it, particularly when they said there would be about a hundred in the audience – that's just too many. Anyway, I said yes and flew into Istanbul at about one in the afternoon for the presentation at four. The plane was on time, but I really regret not arriving the day before, particularly when you think what happened next. I was met at the airport, but there was so much traffic it took us nearly two hours to get to the venue. We arrived with half an hour to spare, whereupon my hosts, in true Turkish style, immediately offered us tea. If only I'd said no, I would have had more time to check everything. As it was, when we connected my laptop, I noticed that none of the images were showing and that my notes didn't show on screen. If only I'd printed them out! By this time we only had five minutes to go and that was when the technician arrived, and he somehow got everything fixed in time. Unfortunately, people kept arriving and it was impossible to start on schedule. In fact, the room was actually far too small, but instead of closing the door, they kept letting people in. I finally started half an hour late. A big part of me wishes I had never agreed, but in fact the audience was so appreciative I'd probably do it again.

▶ 10.02

1 If only she had asked me …
2 Had the weather been better …
3 I should have realised …
4 You might have told me …
5 I really wish I'd been there.
6 He ought to have known …
7 It's about time they …
8 We should never have gone.

▶ 10.03

1 **A** Good luck with your driving test. I hope you pass this time!
  B Thanks, it would definitely be a case of third time lucky though, wouldn't it?
2 **A** Aren't you going to have a second go at becoming team leader?
  B Well, I'm not sure. I think I might be tempting fate if I tried again.
3 **A** Have you got your exam results yet?
  B No, but fingers crossed I've been successful this time.
4 **A** That restaurant you've booked looks really expensive.
  B Don't worry, I've taken out extra cash just to be on the safe side.
5 **A** I hear you're going skiing. Be careful you don't break anything.
  B Well, touch wood; I've been skiing for over ten years and never had an injury yet!

▶ 10.04

a Acorns protect you from lightning strikes.
b People claim that ladybirds bring good luck.
c The four-leaf clover is a plant which brings good fortune.
d This charm bracelet brings strength and happiness.
e I have a rabbit's foot in my sports bag.

▶ 10.05

A So, thanks for coming, Anthony. We were very interested in your proposal.
B So perhaps you could start by …
C Sorry, but could I have a glass of water?
B Of course. Here you are.
A Now as I was saying, we are very interested in your ideas and wanted to find out some more.
C Where … ?
A Please, after you …
C I was just going to ask – where would you like me to start?
A Ah, well, I understand that you train people in making presentations.
C That's true, but, before we go on, can I just say that my main job is acting? I do a wide range of radio and TV shows. Theatre as well, obviously.
B Sorry to interrupt, but will we have seen you on TV?
C Possibly. Four or five years ago. Anyway, as I was saying, I work with politicians and business leaders to help them give more effective presentations.
A & B So how …
B Sorry, you first.
A How do you train them?

C Well, we work a lot on posture, breathing, relaxation, some voice drills and so on.
A Speaking of posture, is it an important part of the training?
C Yes, in fact we warm up with a lot of posture exercises, which allow us to have better control over our bodies. It's a technique a lot of actors use.
A Thanks. Do go on.
C Where was I?

▶ 10.06

1 You can't give me a hand, can you?
2 It was a great film, wasn't it?
3 He's not available, is he?
4 That's your bag, isn't it?
5 That wasn't your phone, was it?
6 You can speak German, can't you?
7 That wasn't our flight, was it?
8 It won't hurt, will it?
9 Your boss is coming, isn't he?
10 It isn't time already, is it?

▶ 10.07

LOUIS Are you enjoying the conference, Christina?
CHRISTINA Well, so far not really, to be honest, Louis. I've seen some truly awful talks, and I've got so much work to do back at the school, part of me wishes I hadn't come.
L That's a shame! I saw a couple of fantastic presentations this morning. The best one was a workshop demonstrating a new approach to reading tasks in the classroom; I'm going to try it with my students next week.
C Maybe I've just made bad choices about which sessions to attend then. This guy this morning was meant to be talking about managing challenging behaviour in the classroom, but for a start he read his presentation out word for word, which is always a recipe for disaster. Honestly, wouldn't you think that someone at a teachers' conference would know better than that? And then he went into so much tedious detail that, by the end of it all, quite apart from the fact that I was practically dropping off from boredom, I couldn't really tell you what he'd actually said.
L That sounds really poor. You really need to summarise your main points at the end, don't you?
C Yes, if he'd done that, I might have got more from it, I suppose. And then the other talk I went to was by this course book author who was totally self-obsessed, and her whole talk was about selling some idea to do with vocabulary learning that's evidently the main focus of her new book. It was just a blatant attempt to sell more of her books. Also, she kept making these throwaway remarks to her mates in the audience; little jokes that none of the rest of us could understand; it was awful.
L I really think you've been unlucky. The sessions I've attended have all been really well presented and relevant. I feel like I'm going to go back to work buzzing with new ideas.
C Well, that's great! That's why we go to conferences, isn't it? So have you got anything in mind for tomorrow? You're obviously better at predicting what's going to be worth hearing.
L I thought maybe the thing by Selma Green on using digital media in the classroom. I've not heard her before, but she's reported to be an excellent speaker.
C Oh yes, I saw her at a conference in Milan last year, and she had the audience eating out of her hand. I was with a group of colleagues, and we couldn't stop talking about her presentation all evening. There was so much food for thought there. Yes, I'll definitely join you for that one. And what about the slot after coffee? Do you have a recommendation for that?
L Well, as it happens, I do. It's this really interesting guy talking about his unusual views on teaching grammar. Well worth a listen.
C What's his name? Will I have heard of him?
L Oh, you've definitely heard of him. In fact, you're talking to him now!

ANSWER KEY

Unit 1

1A

1

a 2 extremely 3 clearly 4 apparently 5 widely 6 effectively 7 Unfortunately

b 2 Your English will improve rapidly if you listen to music and watch films.
3 A lot of language schools have opened in the last ten years in England.
4 You lived in Bangkok, so presumably you speak Thai fluently.
5 For adult learners, listening is usually the hardest skill.
6 I almost never write down new vocabulary.

2

a 2 ear 3 at 4 picked 5 struggled 6 accustomed 7 rusty 8 conversation

3

a 2 dedication 3 Motivation 4 interaction 5 distractions 6 competence
7 reluctance 8 interference

1B

1

a 2 will have been studying 3 hadn't found 4 have tried
5 have never written 6 has been revising

b 2 'll have been 3 Have you ever had 4 have 5 've always enjoyed
6 've applied 7 has got 8 'd just arrived 9 've got 10 'll have made

2

a 2 ongoing 3 barely 4 way 5 increase 6 substantially 7 rapid 8 subtle
9 shift 10 changes

3

a 2 studying 3 tried 4 practising 5 working 6 revising

1C

1

a 2 loads of 3 Give or take 4 Whatshisname 5 something to do with
6 Somewhere in the region of 7 words to that effect

c 2 d 3 b 4 a 5 f 6 c

2

a 1 /iː/: green, believe
2 /e/: instead, bread
3 /eɪ/: break, great
4 /eə/ wear, bear
5 /ɪə/ pier, career
6 /ɜː/: earn, learn

1D

1

a True: 1, 2, 5; False: 3, 4, 6

b Direct: 3, 6, 7
Softened: 2, 4, 5, 8

2

a 2 I disagree. However, you've got a point about the price of transport.
3 I'm in two minds about this. I'm not sure if you are right or not.
4 I don't really get what the fuss is about. In my opinion, Edinburgh is cheap.
5 You're spot on there! Listening is really tricky. Keep practising.
6 I agree with the others up to a point, but I think speaking is harder.
Good luck!
7 You are all missing the point. Learning English just takes time.
8 I would go along with that. Good discussion, by the way.

3

a Possible answer

I'm in two minds about this. It is interesting to watch lectures from different classes, but it seems to me that if I cannot get feedback from the teachers or even ask questions, it is harder to actually learn.

You are spot on about the short clips, particularly for practical demonstrations of scientific or engineering concepts. But that's nonsense about translating the pages. Most of the translation is automatic and doesn't always work properly. However, you've hit the nail on the head about learning for people in remote regions or those who cannot travel for other reasons.

Overall, I agree that there are a lot of opportunities for us online, but I still think you are better off with a teacher.

Reading and listening extension

1

a a 3 b 5 d 4 e 6 f 2

b 2 speak several languages
3 do not follow
4 come out of
5 for hundreds of years

c True: 1, 2, 6; False: 3, 7; Not enough information: 4, 5, 8

2

a 3

b Zac: 1, 4
Rebecca: 2, 6, 7, 9
Neither: 3, 5, 8, 10

Review and extension

1

2 They were really hoping to stay with us
3 she also knows Turkish
4 You can easily find a shop
5 I recently met the teacher
6 need / necessity
7 limitations
8 noticeable
9 steadily
10 substantial

2

2 She can be very rude – I have to bite my tongue to avoid an argument.
3 When I was a child, my mother fought tooth and nail to get me the best education possible, and she succeeded!
4 I love going shopping with my friend Sandra – she's got a nose for bargains!
5 I recently employed an accountant to manage my money. I'm so glad I did – he's a safe pair of hands.

Unit 2

2A

1

a 2 further 3 darker 4 considerably 5 the most 6 much 7 more
8 significantly

2

a 2 h 3 d 4 f 5 b 6 e 7 a 8 g

b 2 came 3 relate 4 bombarded 5 slipped 6 held 7 brought
8 went on and on

3

2 So did you manage to fit in with all those important people?
3 Overall, I think I did quite well, actually.
4 One man went on and on about the budget.
5 It was a great day and I learned lots.

2B

1

a 2 arrive on 3 hoping to 4 will be 5 is due to 6 plan to take her
7 won't see 8 will be going 9 are thinking of 10 about to

b Definite: Tom's presentation, Sarah's graduation, Tom's call
Definitely not: trip to Victoria
Possible: meeting with Kenzo, trip with Sarah, Kenzo attending conference,
dinner with Antonia

2

a Across: 3 hurtle 5 crawl 6 stagger 7 limp
Down: 2 soar 4 slide 5 creep

b 2 marched 3 zoomed 4 drifting 5 rushed 6 strolling

2C

1

a 2 interests 3 high 4 get 5 want 6 possibility

c 2 e 3 d 4 c 5 b

2

a 2 No, she emailed them last <u>month</u>.
3 No, everyone spoke <u>German</u> during the meeting.
4 No, but the <u>presenters</u> spoke English.
5 No, but I'll be going there for <u>work</u>.
6 No, I think we'll be going to <u>Greece</u>.
7 No, I think I'll be <u>driving</u> there.
8 No, I'm doing a <u>workshop</u> in Berlin.

2D

1

a 3, 6

b 2 b 3 a 4 c 5 c 6 b

2

a 2 Even though 3 On the other hand 4 unlike 5 by comparison
6 alternatively

3

a Possible answer

I live in a village ten kilometres from the nearest town, and the public transport
links are limited. Despite repeated requests, our council has not really
improved things over the last few years. For that reason, I and many others use
cars, which leads to traffic congestion and also makes it more dangerous for
cyclists. There are also a number of elderly people in the village who neither
drive nor cycle.

Even though the station is only three kilometres from the village, it is rarely used
because trains only stop there once an hour. A better timetable would make the
station more popular and reduce the CO_2 emissions from cars. By comparison,
emissions from trains are about half as much per kilometre. Villagers would still
have to drive to the station, but the council might consider making a cycle path,
which would encourage cycling. Alternatively, I would recommend organising a
bus service from the village to the station and also to the nearest town centre.
This would allow the elderly to get into town more frequently.

I realise that all of these plans will cost money. Nevertheless, I feel they
are necessary.

Reading and listening extension

1

a 3

b 2 c 3 a 4 a 5 b

c 2, 3, 5

2

a 1 smell 2 taste 3 uncle 4 doctor

b 2 isn't 3 does 4 didn't 5 is 6 hasn't 7 doesn't know 8 doesn't think

c 1 a, c, d, f
2 a, b, d

Review and extension

1

2 as much as 3 I was hanging around with them more and more
4 more and more quickly 5 the most light 6 I'm going to try to explain / I'll try to
explain 7 leaped / leapt 8 crept 9 slid 10 bombarding

2

2 A friend of mine has just turned down the chance to go on a three-week safari!
I would jump at the chance to have a holiday like that!
3 When I saw my favourite band on stage for the first time, I felt a rush
of excitement!
4 I never thought I'd get married, but last week I decided to take the plunge and
propose to Evelyn. She said yes!
5 There's a nice tapas restaurant nearby – I've never had tapas before, but it
looks good, so I don't mind giving it a whirl.

Unit 3

3A

1

a 2 Seldom 3 Never 4 did I hear them 5 did they start 6 No sooner
7 did I ever think 8 can we really stop

b 2 Not once did I feel I wasn't making a difference.
3 No sooner had we arrived in Bogotá than we were helping kids learn
to read.
4 Not only did we help a lot of people, we also made great friends.
5 No way will I ever forget the things I saw there.
6 Rarely do we get a chance to really help people.

2

a 2 e 3 a 4 c 5 f 6 d

b 2 deprived 3 impoverished 4 destitute 5 within our means 6 disposable
7 making ends meet 8 prosperity

3

a Ooo: charity, poverty, destitute, relatives, everyone
oOo: enrolment, requirement, improvement, nutritious
ooO: volunteer

3B

1

a 2 b 3 h 4 e 5 g 6 a 7 c 8 d

b 2 earning 3 had 4 had been 5 was doing 6 had 7 would
8 would 9 was 10 would 11 hospitalised 12 was to start

2

a 2 e 3 d 4 h 5 a 6 f 7 b 8 g

b 2 rich 3 coastline 4 face 5 wooded 6 dense 7 empty 8 sand

3

a /t/ pronounced: biggest egg, What a, can't ask, great in
/t/ not pronounced: can't find, it's so, biggest fish, great cook

3C

1

a 2 In a nutshell 3 In other words 4 to cut a long story short
5 what I meant was

c 2 to cut a long story short 3 what I meant was 4 to put it another way
5 in other words 6 that is to say

2

a 2 e 3 g 4 a 5 f 6 b 7 c 8 d

3D

1

a True: 1, 3, 6; False: 4, 5; Not enough information: 2

b 2 by boat 3 cruise 4 traffic jams 5 buildings 6 negotiate

2

a 2 freshly baked 3 stunning views 4 absolutely delicious 5 heart-stopping
6 excellent value for money 7 breathtaking 8 highly recommended

3

a Possible answer

Henley-on-Thames is a beautiful Oxfordshire town on the River Thames about 60 kilometres from London. With a population of around 10,000, it is an easy place to visit on foot. I arrived by train from London and the journey only took about an hour.

The White Fox was within walking distance of both the station and the town centre, and we had stunning views of the river. Fortunately, we were not there during the world-famous regatta, when every room in the town is booked.

The room was small but very clean and the staff were extremely friendly. Our only complaint was the low water pressure in the shower, but the receptionist was quick to change our room. We ate in the restaurant's modern dining room, which was tastefully furnished in a contemporary style. The food was mouthwatering, all made from locally produced ingredients. It was also very good value for money!

After a breakfast of freshly baked bread and homemade jam, we had time to visit the sights. These included the 200-year-old bridge, a 700-year-old inn and a stately home just outside the town in the rolling English countryside. We thoroughly enjoyed our stay.

Reading and listening extension

1

a 1 The author loves his work because he is adventurous.
2 Doing expedition medicine is very different from working in a hospital.
3 The author thinks that all doctors would benefit from working on an expedition.

b 2 a 3 c 4 c 5 a 6 b

2

a 1 b 2 b

b 1 d 2 b 3 c 4 a

c True: 2, 5, 6, 8; False: 1, 7; Not enough information: 3, 4

Review and extension

1

2 Not only were the staff   3 was going to notice / would notice
4 should confidential documents be   5 when we needed
6 something awful was going to happen   7 Never before have we received
8 Only then will I   9 when the bus broke down   10 wilderness
11 wooded slopes   12 rainforest

2

2 I found maths really difficult at school. I tried really hard, but it was an uphill struggle.
3 My cat has been really ill, but the vet has told us that she is out of the woods. The kids will be happy!
4 My husband is really stressed – he's swamped at the moment.
5 My sister's really good at looking at a problem and seeing a solution – I just get bogged down.

Unit 4

4A

1

a 2 Her recently published book, *Staying Alive*, is a complete A–Z of health and fitness.
3 Getting people of all ages to eat and drink sensibly has become her life's work.
4 Her rags-to-riches life story is living proof that dreams can come true.
5 Her easy-to-follow keep-fit apps top sales charts all over the world.

b 2 that perfectly judged shot
3 the climate change problem
4 anything like a Thai green curry / something like a Thai green curry
5 my uncle's life's work
6 plenty to do

2

a 2 think it over 3 rational 4 gut instinct 5 on impulse
6 subconsciously 7 spontaneous 8 think twice

c 2 self-conscious 3 conscientious 4 sensitive 5 rational
6 self-confident 7 money-conscious 8 sensible

4B

1

a 2 d 3 g 4 a 5 b 6 c 7 f 8 e

b 2 to send 3 had it extended 4 to help 5 had it made 6 draw
7 our post forwarded 8 set up

2

a 2 triggers 3 a lasting memory 4 treasure 5 a vivid memory
6 slipped 7 come to mind 8 painful memory

b 2 memory 3 comes 4 souvenirs 5 vague 6 recall 7 forget
8 refresh 9 treasure

3

a 2 We <u>a</u>lways went on <u>h</u>oliday to <u>I</u>taly.
3 In the <u>eve</u>ning, we would <u>walk</u> by the <u>lake</u>.
4 My <u>bro</u>thers put me in a <u>row</u>ing boat.
5 I <u>still</u> have my <u>photo</u> album to re<u>fresh</u> my <u>memory</u>.

4C

1

a 2 No offence intended
3 I see where you're coming from
4 I beg to differ
5 With all due respect
6 OK, I take your point
7 In fact, if you don't mind me saying so

c 2 You're telling me.
3 With all due respect, you've only just started.
4 I take your point, but you're still very new. /You're still very new, but I take your point.
5 If you don't mind me saying so, it's probably best to wait. / It's probably best to wait, if you don't mind me saying so.
6 You've hit the nail on the head.

2

a 2 aloud 3 died 4 break 5 weak 6 hear 7 blue 8 sail

4D

1

a True: 2, 3, 5, 6, False: 1, 4, 7, 8

b 2 He was born in Vicenza, Italy.
3 He started speaking English when the family moved to England.
4 He went to South Africa to attend school and play more rugby.
5 He moved to France to play rugby for Perpignan.
6 He played his first full game for Italy.
7 He played for Italy against Scotland.

2

a Immediate: 2
Short interval: 3, 4, 6
Long interval: 5

3

a Possible answer

I met Robin down by the River Thames. We sat on a bench watching barges pass slowly by. The sun was out, and it didn't take long before he was chatting away about life touring as a guitarist. I wanted to know how he had become such an amazing musician. 'Well, I'm sure it's in my blood, since both my dad and my uncle are musicians – my uncle has played professionally all his life and is still performing and composing.' He seems quietly confident of his own ability but highlights some of the disadvantages of his chosen profession. On European or American tours, there will be a show each day, which means travelling and practising as well as sound checking every single day. 'Hotel rooms are fun at first, but after a while you miss your own home,' he adds.

When I ask him how he got into music in the first place, his face lights up. 'There was always music at home – I have two brothers and a sister, and we all played a lot of different instruments. We had different bands featuring combinations of family or friends. It wasn't until I was about 15, though, that I realised I would like to have a career in music.' Having studied music at university, Robin got his first break replacing his uncle at a small festival in Norway. 'The moment I played live with the band I realised what a great feeling it can be.' Shortly after that, a chance meeting with a drummer led to an offer of work with another band, closely followed by a chance to accompany Hugh Jones on tour. And the rest, as they say, is history.

Reading and listening extension

1

a 1 rational   2 mental   3 poor   4 useful   5 better

b a 3   b 7   d 6   e 2   f 5   g 4

c 2 c   3 a   4 c   5 b   6 b

2

a 2 twelve   3 cake   4 memory   5 music   6 brain   7 South America   8 husband

b Yes: 2, 3, 4, 8
No: 5, 6, 7

Review and extension

1

2 The group's first day
3 the number of personal computers
4 get the job done on time
5 old people
6 rational
7 sensitive
8 self-confident
9 sensible
10 conscious

2

2 Thanks for letting me know that you enjoy role play – I'll bear that in mind for the next lesson.
3 If you don't agree with an action, you must speak your mind; otherwise, things will never change.
4 I can't believe how angry my friend is with me. She hates dancing, so it never crossed my mind to invite her to my party!
5 You should have told me you wanted me to buy chocolate – I can't read your mind.

Unit 5

5A

1

a 2 whose   3 where   4 all of whom   5 who   6 why   7 which
8 the result of which

b 2 h   3 g   4 b   5 d   6 c   7 e   8 a

2

a 2 goods   3 assault   4 community   5 solitary   6 life   7 psychiatric
8 convicted   9 sentences   10 served

b 2 sentenced   3 serve   4 reduced   5 counselling   6 victims

3

a /s/: person, dismiss
/ʃ/: mission, Russian, passion, pressure
/ʒ/: occasion, Asian, collision
/z/: imprisonment, cousin

5B

1

a 2 aren't really expected   3 was required   4 is called on   5 is essential
6 English is mandatory   7 must do   8 should be

b 2 expected   3 have to   4 mandatory   5 essential   6 you have
7 expected   8 requirement

2

a Across: 2 energy   4 financial   8 tourism   9 public   10 industrial
Down: 1 transport   3 manufacturing   5 agricultural   6 construction   7 retail

3

a Oo: 2, 4
oO: 3, 5, 6

5C

1

a 2 hazard   3 Presumably   4 stands   5 memory   6 impression

b 2 c   3 f   4 e   5 a   6 b

d Speculating: 3, 4, 6, 7, 9
Recalling: 2, 5, 8

2

a 2 Some countries simply <u>copy</u> … while other countries <u>create</u>.
3 It's not just the <u>money</u> … it's the time <u>and</u> the money.
4 I don't know <u>any</u> jokes … I don't know any <u>good</u> jokes anyway.
5 The lesson wasn't just <u>difficult</u> … it was difficult <u>and</u> boring.

5D

1

a 2 sometimes   3 online profile   4 automatically   5 odd
6 complete an assignment   7 uncomfortable for interviewees   8 cautious

b a 5   b 4   c 1   d 2   e 3

2

a 2 In addition   3 As well as   4 above   5 Besides   6 Moreover

3

a Possible answer

It is fair to say that the job market today is difficult because there are fewer jobs and more candidates for each good position. Furthermore, globalisation has meant that candidates can apply from a lot further away than was the case in the past. In this essay, I will outline what you need to do in terms of online presence to ensure you are as well prepared as possible in the job market.

The first thing you need to do is to keep your online profile up to date. Besides ensuring that all the information is in one place, you'll allow potential employers to find you without your needing to apply. In addition to including professional and academic information, you should check the words you use because sophisticated search engines look for them when looking for candidates.

Not only is it advisable to keep your online profile looking as professional as possible, but you should also limit your social online presence, particularly if friends regularly tag you at parties. Furthermore, it is worth checking that your preferences are set as privately as possible so you do not reveal too much publicly.

My final suggestion would be to comment and write on the Internet in a way that you feel is appropriate and in a way that you are happy for others to see. Besides comments and posts, email and blogs are also important mediums to watch out for.

Overall, I would say that an online presence is a must in the current job market, but it is clearly something you have to regularly update.

Reading and listening extension

1

a 3

b 3, 4, 5

c 2 eager   3 relieved   4 difficult   5 calmer   6 behaviour

2

a 1 a police officer   2 an engineer   3 a fruit picker

b 2 Adriana   3 Adriana   4 Ben   5 Martina   6 Ben, Martina
7 Martina   8 Martina

c 2 Some   3 not easy   4 less   5 still has to   6 misses   7 is   8 doesn't work
9 doesn't think   10 doesn't work

Review and extension

1

2 the date on which
3 your email in which
4 the details of which
5 whoever finds my money
6 wherever they like
7 all of whom / who all
8 construction
9 sector
10 commit a crime
11 retail
12 manufacturing

2

2 I always know when my nephew is up to no good because he suddenly goes quiet.
3 My neighbour never punishes her children. They get away with murder.
4 With children, you've got to lay down the law right from the start.
5 Ever since she was mugged, my aunt's been looking over her shoulder. She's worried it will happen again.

Unit 6
6A
1

a 2 I've lived 3 I'm doing 4 been doing 5 Do you think 6 insist
7 be studying 8 Are you 9 I need 10 I'm looking 11 is recruiting

b 2 e 3 c 4 b 5 f 6 h 7 a 8 d

2

a 2 powerful 3 observant 4 iconic 5 humorous 6 bleak 7 elaborate
8 flawless

b 2 elaborate 3 gritty 4 playful 5 repetitive 6 powerful 7 iconic
8 meaningful

d 1 extremely 2 pretty 3 incredibly 4 utterly 5 rather

6B
1

a 2 h 3 f 4 a 5 b 6 c 7 d 8 e

b 2 looking 3 waiting 4 Pausing 5 crackling 6 Brushing 7 frightened
8 Sensing 9 having considered 10 Having completed

2

a 2 e 3 f 4 h 5 a 6 g 7 d 8 b

b 2 ashamed 3 insecure 4 jealous 5 overjoyed 6 satisfied
7 overexcited 8 frustrated

3

a 2 She was so <u>disillusioned</u>. 3 I was absolutely <u>petrified</u>.
4 I was <u>absolutely</u> petrified. 5 I felt <u>extremely</u> frustrated.
6 I felt extremely <u>frustrated</u>. 7 They were <u>very</u> jealous.
8 They were very <u>jealous</u>. 9 I'm really <u>ashamed</u>. 10 I'm <u>really</u> ashamed.

6C
1

a a 2, 12 b 3, 8 c 4, 5, 6, 11 d 7, 9 e 10, 11

b 2 is clear 3 First and foremost, perspective 4 perfectly obvious, talk
5 Moving on, turn 6 table, take 7 in conclusion, specifically 8 recap
9 elaborate

2

a 2 3 ↗ 4 ↗ 5 ↘ 6 ↘ 7 ↗ 8 ↗

6D
1

a True: 2, 3, 5, 6, 8; False: 1, 4, 7

b a 7 b 2 c 6 d 4 e 5 f 3

2

a 2 I am writing 3 appeared 4 fit 5 experience 6 good 7 completion
8 raised 9 hope 10 interesting 11 attaching 12 Kind regards,

3

a Possible answer

Dear Sir/Madam,

I am writing in reply to your advertisement posted in last week's issue. I am an enthusiastic cinema goer, and I would be delighted to be considered for the position.

I am currently studying Italian and drama at Queen's University, and my dissertation is on the treatment of modern literature in Italian cinema. This has led me to spend a lot of time not only watching Italian films, but analysing them, too – something I have thoroughly enjoyed.

My knowledge of international cinema is substantial and I am a regular reader of *Film Monthly*. During my last holiday, I was lucky enough to spend four weeks working on a film set on location in Cork, which gave me a valuable insight into cinematography.

I am a competent writer and have already had a number of articles published on the Film Society website. Please find attached some examples.

The other reason for my interest is that I hope to embark on a career in journalism once I have graduated. Therefore, I would really welcome any opportunity to add to my writing portfolio.

I trust you will give my application your consideration. I look forward to hearing from you. Please find attached my CV.

Yours faithfully,

Reading and listening extension
1

a 2

b a 4 b 6 c 2 e 7 f 5 g 3

c True: 1, 3, 6, 7; False: 2, 4; Not enough information: 5, 8

2

a 1 Lewis 2 Martha 3 earthquake 4 drama 5 30

b 2 a 3 c 4 b 5 a 6 b

Review and extension
1

2 increased 3 Not having been 4 Having experienced it
5 not knowing where to go 6 get frustrated 7 make other people jealous
8 I would be devastated 9 feel insecure 10 in a humorous way

2

2 I went to a wedding last weekend and the bride's dress was bright green – I couldn't believe my eyes!
3 When I was a little girl, my parents told me we were going on a plane to visit my grandparents. I was over the moon!
4 One of my colleagues tells jokes all the time, and they're not very funny ones. It really gets on my nerves.
5 I told my friend I'd go to a dance class with her. I don't like dancing, but I'll grin and bear it if it makes her happy.

Unit 7
7A
1

a 2 h 3 f 4 b 5 d 6 g 7 e 8 c

b 2 could have 3 couldn't have 4 it's likely that 5 may well
6 almost certainly 7 there's a reasonable chance 8 bound

2

a 2 warm-hearted 3 heartwarming 4 half-hearted 5 hard-hearted
6 open-minded 7 narrow-minded 8 heartbreaking

b 2 d 3 g 4 e 5 c 6 b 7 a

7B
1

a 2 a 3 e 4 h 5 g 6 f 7 d 8 b

b 2 It was a former student of mine who first told me about it.
3 All I wanted was to relax on a sunny beach.
4 What I absolutely love about it is the incredible atmosphere.
5 What is (just) amazing is (just) how friendly the locals are.
6 What happens is you go into a café and people just start talking to you.
7 To be honest, it's only when I'm there that I'm really happy.
8 What really annoys me is I've tried really hard, but I can't get a job there.

2

a 2 collaboration 3 isolation 4 innovation 5 tolerant 6 perspectives
7 self-awareness 8 optimism

b 2 distribution 3 materialism 4 selfishness 5 capitalism 6 ostracism

3

a 2 The <u>reason</u> I'm here is to help you.
3 The <u>one</u> thing I cannot do is cook.
4 What went <u>wrong</u> was I lost my ticket and got fined.
5 The <u>main</u> reason I cycle to work is to save money.
6 The <u>only</u> thing I ask is that you try your best.
7 What will <u>happen</u> is someone will be waiting with your name on a sign.
8 What they <u>proposed</u> was impossible to deliver.

7C

1

a a 4 c 2 d 3, 5

b 2 apologise 3 tactful 4 take 5 inexcusable 6 came 7 overreacted

2

a 1 would, could
2 through
3 bough, announce, south
4 although, dough
5 brought, four, thought
6 tough, southern
7 cough
8 conscious

7D

1

a True: 1, 3, 6; False: 2, 4, 5

b 2 b 3 c 4 c 5 a 6 a

2

a 2 specifically 3 such as 4 in particular 5 demonstrated 6 namely

3

a Possible answer

This proposal outlines some ideas for improving the way we are currently
learning English. Feedback from classmates and our teacher suggests that
there is one skill we would all like to improve, namely speaking. We all agree
that we need to change the focus of our learning, specifically to prepare in the
daytime outside class, so we can benefit more from our evening lessons with
the teacher.

Successful lessons this term, for instance the presentations project, worked
well because they were well planned by the participants and based around
topics we are familiar with but don't always discuss in English. Students were
motivated by these classes, as demonstrated by the attendance that week, and
this is proof that we should take this direction more often.

My first suggestion is to have one of our two lessons each week focused
entirely on speaking, with content and themes chosen by the students, and
the other one reserved for more traditional subjects, specifically grammar and
vocabulary. Other skills, such as reading and listening, could be done at home
at our own pace, and activities that require marking, such as essay writing,
could be submitted every two weeks. A class of 12 is a good size, and we all
are at advanced level, so I would also recommend more collaboration on
writing tasks.

I am confident that this approach would be more motivating, make better use
of our teacher and result in better lessons because they would rely more on
student input. I look forward to discussing this proposal in more detail.

Reading and listening extension

1

a 1 c 2 a 3 d 4 b

b True: 1, 2, 3, 8; False: 4, 5, 6, 7

c 4, 7

2

a 2, 4, 7, 8, 9

b 2 in addition to 3 sad 4 can barely cope with 5 doesn't believe
6 difficult 7 speaks 8 doesn't think

82

Review and extension

2 quite possible 3 likely 4 forgotten is the 5 amazing was that
6 heartbreaking 7 absent-minded 8 mouthwatering 9 loneliness
10 innovation(s) 11 intimacy 12 cold

2 self-aware 3 self-sacrificing 4 self-sufficient 5 self-centred

Unit 8

8A

1

a 2 sleepwalking 3 to be 4 doing 5 walking 6 acting 7 to create
8 to wake up 9 to talk 10 to need 11 moving

b 2 putting 3 do 4 decide 5 not having been given 6 to alter
7 hearing 8 having waited 9 to meet 10 complaining

2

a

		¹L	I	G	H	T	
	²T	U	R	N			
³O	V	E	R	S	L	E	E	P
		⁴L	O	G			
⁵D	R	E	A	M			
			⁶N	A	P		
	⁷W	I	D	E			
	⁸F	A	S	T			

b 2 log 3 fast 4 off 5 nap 6 light 7 off 8 wide 9 oversleep

3

a 2 <u>sleep</u> like a <u>log</u>
3 <u>fast</u> a<u>sleep</u>
4 <u>have</u> a <u>nap</u>
5 <u>wide</u> a<u>wake</u>
6 <u>don't</u> over<u>sleep</u>

8B

1

a 2 e 3 c 4 a 5 b 6 f

b 2 just in case 3 provided that 4 Assuming 5 should 6 weren't
7 on condition 8 Suppose

2

a 2 saggy 3 wrinkles 4 dry 5 thinning 6 ageing 7 Moisturise
8 tighten 9 balanced 10 weight 11 glowing 12 circulation
13 heart 14 cardiovascular

b 2 plastic 3 strengthening 4 toning 5 tightened 6 firmer 7 glow
8 regular 9 balanced

3

a 1 three will do 2 or a fork 3 just a little 4 around 30 grams
5 about 10 grams 6 the eggs 7 probably a minute

8C

1

a 2 prepared 3 hoping 4 the question 5 say 6 offer 7 authorised
8 way 9 issue 10 flexible

b 2 I'm not in a position to accept anything less.
3 The rug is worth much more than that.
4 Is that your final offer?
5 Could you see your way to increasing that offer a little?
6 I was hoping for a hotel room in the region of $100 a night.

c Buying: 2, 5, 7, 9
Selling: 3, 4, 6, 8

2

a Statement: 4, 6, 7, 10, 11
Question: 2, 3, 5, 8, 9, 12

8D

1

a 2 a 3 c 4 c 5 b 6 c

b 2 chill out 3 old and new 4 worked there for a while
5 organically produced 6 international

2

a 2 state-of-the-art 3 deep 4 lovingly 5 stunning 6 romantic

3

a Possible answer

Fresh fish grilling on a barbecue? The sound of waves crashing onto a beach? Tales of pirates and smugglers from the olden days? If you like the sound of this, then head to our guesthouse on the cliffs near Polperro, Cornwall.

For over 200 years, we have been offering hospitality to weary travellers. In a stunning location high above the sea, we are uniquely placed to offer great walks, fascinating history and a wide range of sports and activities.

Family-owned for the last 80 years, the Red Manor is a cosy guesthouse and a gastronomic experience all at the same time. Serving fresh fish and seafood, barbecued on the beach in good weather, we are loved by locals and visitors alike. Our recently renovated bedrooms with power showers and memory foam mattresses are spacious and offer panoramic sea views. Whatever the time of year, you will love what we have to offer, from roaring fires in the winter to watching gorgeous sunsets in the summer.

Sounds tempting, doesn't it? Don't delay. Book today. Great value deals available now.

Reading and listening extension

1

a 2 forced 3 hang 4 find 5 say 6 experiencing 7 use 8 accompany
9 spend

b True: 1, 3, 4, 8; False: 5, 7; Not enough information: 2, 6

2

a 1 70 2 3 3 60 4 64

b 2 time to do what he wants 3 without payment 4 appreciates
5 may decide 6 bad-tempered

c 2 c 3 a 4 c 5 b 6 b

Review and extension

1

2 to be working 3 otherwise 4 If I had enough money, I'd come
5 If 6 it would take me / it'd take me
7 ways of communicating / means of communication
8 Being appreciated / Feeling appreciated 9 get 10 broke out in
11 preventing 12 saggy / wrinkly / less firm / wrinkled 13 showing

2

2 I've just started ballet classes. They're supposed to be for adult beginners, but I'm far and away the worst there!
3 The doctor says the pain in my knee is from wear and tear, so there's not much he can do.
4 I didn't do much last weekend – just bits and pieces around the house, like vacuuming.
5 My children argue all the time. I'm sick and tired of it.

Unit 9

9A

1

a 2 myself 3 yourself 4 herself 5 himself 6 one another's 7 ourselves
8 yourselves 9 themselves

b 2 himself 3 each other 4 relaxing 5 by themselves 6 her
7 each other 8 myself

2

a 2 regain 3 recreates 4 restore 5 redevelop/regenerate 6 rejuvenated
7 regenerate/redevelop 8 renovated

b 2 restored 3 redeveloping 4 renovation 5 re-establish 6 rejuvenated
7 recreated 8 has regained

9B

1

a 2 then Newcastle 3 never did 4 weren't 5 never 6 didn't

b 2 b 3 e 4 a 5 f 6 c

2

a 2 innovative 3 nondescript 4 over the top 5 tasteless 6 graceful
7 out of place 8 imposing 9 stunning

b Across: 4 housing estate 7 mansion 9 warehouse 10 studio
Down: 1 bungalow 2 cabin 3 power 5 skyscraper 6 semi-detached
8 penthouse

3

a Oo: penthouse, mansion, tasteless, graceful, stunning, power
oOo: apartment, imposing
Ooo: skyscraper, nondescript
Oooo: innovative

9C

1

a 2 absolutely 3 full 4 beyond 5 jump 6 right 7 on earth 8 raise
9 consequences 10 investigate

c 2 I have every intention of investigating the matter.
3 There's no reason to raise your voice.
4 You owe me an explanation.
5 I warn you there will be consequences.
6 Words cannot express my utter disbelief.
7 I'd like you to take full responsibility.
8 You've failed to fulfil your responsibilities.

2

a 1 abseil, German 2 baguette, French 3 cello, Italian
4 mosquito, Spanish

9D

1

a 2 a 3 c 4 a 5 c 6 a

b True: 1, 3, 5; False: 2, 4, 6

2

a 2 because of this, 3 Due to 4 As a result of 5 led to 6 Thus,

3

a Possible answer

My local town has a population of around 100,000, but this figure increases by 50% at different times of the year due to the number of students attending the university and the number of tourists visiting the city's attractions. Because of this, the transport system and the shops are seriously overcrowded. This has led to a decrease in revenue for the shops in the town centre compared with neighbouring towns. The town is therefore planning to redevelop its centre to make it more accessible to pedestrians, less crowded and generally more environmentally friendly.

The first step will be to increase the number of parking spaces on the outskirts of town and also the frequency of shuttle buses to the town centre on dedicated bus routes, thereby reducing traffic. Traffic in the centre will be reduced by the construction of a two-kilometre tunnel where only buses will be allowed. As a result, shoppers will be dropped off directly under the new shopping area. Private cars will only be able to drive into the centre on alternate days, which will further reduce traffic. The centre itself will benefit from a new outdoor area where shoppers can relax. This area will have a state-of-the-art roof that can open and close depending on the season.

The whole project will take two years to complete and there is always the risk that shoppers and tourists will avoid the town during this time, thus reducing revenue even more. They may also stay away permanently after this period.

The project will rely on careful planning and local support and it is hoped that the town will relaunch as both a shopping and tourist destination.

Reading and listening extension

1

a a2 b6 c4 d3 f5

b 2a 3c 4b 5a 6b

c True: 3, 5; False: 1, 2, 4, 6

2

a 1

b Ben: 5
Eva: 2, 3, 6, 8
Neither: 4, 7

Review and extension

1

2 enjoyed themselves 3 each other 4 yourself 5 because it was
6 graceful 7 tasteless 8 innovative 9 renovate 10 restoring

2

2 on 3 up 4 around 5 in

Unit 10

10A

1

a True: 2, 5, 7, 8; False: 1, 3, 4, 6

b 2 been 3 would have had 4 not printing 5 not been
6 have started 7 they had given 8 could have gone

2

a 2 Had the weather been <u>better</u> … 3 I <u>should</u> have realised …
4 You <u>might</u> have told me … 5 I <u>really</u> wish I'd been there.
6 He <u>ought</u> to have known … 7 It's about <u>time</u> they …
8 We should <u>never</u> have gone.

3

a 2a 3b 4e 5c

b 2 illustrated 3 on 4 demonstrated 5 presented 6 the finer details
7 concluded 8 tribute 9 remarks

10B

1

a 2 claimed 3 been said 4 been proved 5 being generally viewed
6 considered 7 is known 8 thought to 9 have originated
10 been perceived

b 2 have thought 3 are 4 was 5 are known 6 is 7 have been shown
8 said

2

a 2 fate 3 crossed 4 safe 5 wood

c 2 convinced 3 plausible 4 far-fetched 5 persuasive 6 dubious

3

a b5 c6 d6 e4

10C

1

a 2 as I was saying 3 after you 4 before we go on 5 Sorry to interrupt
6 you first 7 Speaking of 8 Do go on

c **Take a turn:** Can I ask a quick question?; Sorry to interrupt, but …;
Speaking of X, …
Pass a turn: Perhaps you could start by …; You first.
Signal that you want to continue: Before we go on, …; As I was saying, …;
Where was I?

2

a 2↘ 3↗ 4↘ 5↗ 6↘ 7↗ 8↗ 9↘ 10↗

10D

1

a 2, 3, 4, 8

b 2c 3c 4b 5a 6c 7b 8b

2

a 2 In *Little Women*, independent and determined Jo dreams of becoming a
successful author.
3 Realising that he has no family left, Tom Hanks's character in *News of the
World* returns to find the girl he saved.
4 Born in New York City, Scarlett Johansson has filmmaking in her blood –
her grandfather was a screenwriter.
5 Having special powers, The Avengers are able to defeat Thanos and save
the universe.
6 *Parasite*, released in the USA in 2019, was the first non-English language
film to win a Best Picture Oscar.

3

a Possible answer

I recently saw a film called *Gone Girl*, which is based on the best-selling novel
by Gillian Flynn. It is a very tense thriller with some quite shocking scenes,
which some people will find too graphic.

It is essentially the story of a marriage told by both leading characters: the
husband, Nick, and the wife, Amy. Nick runs a bar in a small town, financed by
his wife with money from her trust fund. As a child, her parents had published
picture books with a character named 'Amazing Amy' based on her, and this is
worth remembering as the story unwinds. Is the real Amy living out a story she
has invented? At the start of the film, Amy is missing and, as in many missing
person cases, the husband is the prime suspect. There is a lot to dislike about
him, whereas she appears to be the perfect wife. The plot twists and turns and
you are never really sure which of the two is telling the truth.

The ending of the film is a little disappointing, but the picture of a marriage
slowly falling apart is very well narrated. Tension is maintained throughout
by a very good director, David Fincher. Both leading actors, Ben Affleck and
Rosamund Pike, are superbly believable.

If you like gritty, psychological thrillers, you will thoroughly enjoy this film. But
don't watch it if you like happy endings.

Reading and listening extension

1

a 2 doesn't take 3 unrealistic 4 sarcastic 5 impolite

b True: 1, 4, 7, 10; False: 2, 3, 5, 6, 8, 9

2

a 3, 4, 6, 7

b 2c 3a 4b 5c 6c

Review and extension

1

2 Pelé is regarded as / People regard Pelé as
3 It was announced that the price of oil would be / They announced that the price
of oil would be
4 they spoke
5 ought to / should
6 have liked
7 had known, would have
8 convinced / sure
9 plausible
10 traditional
11 upgraded
12 presented

2

2 chances 3 lucky 4 chance 5 luck

Vox pop video

Unit 1

a 2 c   3 a   4 a   5 a   6 a   7 b

b 2 an understanding of people in other countries   3 to practise their English
4 advantages   5 Lauren   6 Lauren

c 2 d   3 e   4 b   5 c

Unit 2

a 2 f   3 e   4 b   5 a   6 d

b 2 a   3 b   4 b   5 b

c 2 Graham   3 Adelaide   4 Laurence   5 Graham

Unit 3

a 2 she has free time   3 in the countryside   4 likes the challenge of   5 hot
6 buildings   7 food and cooking

b 2 c   3 b   4 a   5 b   6 a   7 b   8 c

c 2 f   3 e   4 c   5 a   6 b   7 d

Unit 4

a 2 d   3 e   4 f   5 b   6 a   7 c

b 2 c   3 b   4 a   5 a   6 c   7 b

c 2 sometimes   3 initial   4 shouldn't   5 an instinctive   6 in favour

Unit 5

a 2 b   3 c   4 a   5 a   6 b

b 2 certain people   3 location   4 workplace training   5 not enough jobs
6 could do more

c 2 Stuart   3 Rachel   4 Anna   5 Rachel   6 Everyone

Unit 6

a 2 disagree   3 at home   4 shares   5 to take   6 like
7 keen photographers   8 on special occasions

b 2 e   3 c   4 b   5 a

c 2 a   3 b   4 a   5 c   6 c

Unit 7

a 2 b   3 c   4 a   5 a   6 b

b 2 waiting   3 secretly   4 try different things   5 sociable   6 inward

c 2 c   3 d   4 b   5 a

Unit 8

a 2 know   3 disagrees   4 pollution   5 will need   6 recovering from

b 2 a   3 c   4 b   5 c

c 2 d   3 a   4 e   5 b

Unit 9

a 2 visitors   3 contradicts himself   4 increased   5 worsened   6 Alex

b 2 a   3 c   4 a   5 a   6 c   7 c

c 2 e   3 d   4 b   5 c

Unit 10

a 2 b   3 e   4 a   5 c

b 2 know why things happen   3 wealthy   4 consult an expert   5 global
6 similar

c 2 c   3 a   4 c   5 c   6 b

Acknowledgements

The authors and publishers acknowledge the following sources of copyright material and are grateful for the permissions granted. While every effort has been made, it has not always been possible to identify the sources of all the material used, or to trace all copyright holders. If any omissions are brought to our notice, we will be happy to include the appropriate acknowledgements on reprinting and in the next update to the digital edition, as applicable.

Key:
U = Unit

Photographs:
All the photographs are sourced from Getty Images.

U1: PeopleImages/E+; GoldenKB/iStock/Getty Images Plus; Tetra Images; Kali9/E+; Chaay_Tee/iStock/Getty Images Plus; Shapecharge/E+; **U2:** Anant Agarwal/500Px Plus; Iammotos/iStock/Getty Images Plus; AscentXmedia/E+; Inside Creative House/iStock/Getty Images Plus; Tan Dao Duy/Moment; Georgeclerk/E+; **U3:** Godong/Universal Images Group; Brent Olson/Moment; MangoStar_Studio/iStock/Getty Images Plus; Waitforlight/Moment/Getty Images Plus; Tim Graham/Getty Images News; Bettmann, **U4:** RossHelen/iStock/Getty Images Plus; Enviromantic/E+; Michele D'Amico supersky77/Moment; Pixelfit/E+; FILIPPO MONTEFORTE/AFP; Travelpix Ltd/Stone; lechatnoir/E+; **U5:** FG Trade/E+; Rbouwman/iStock/Getty Images Plus; SOPA Images/LightRocket; Peter Dazeley/The Image Bank; Aydinmutlu/E+; **U6:** Igor Ustynskyy/Moment; Manakin/iStock/Getty Images Plus; Zoltan Glass / Stringer/Picture Post; Zoka74/iStock/Getty Images Plus; Gradyreese/E+; Cecilie_Arcurs/E+; Bertrand Rindoff Petroff/French Select; Ali Jadallah/Anadolu Agency; **U7:** Monkeybusinessimages/iStock/Getty Images Plus; Danita Delimont/Gallo Images/Getty Images Plus; Jose Fuste Raga/Corbis Documentary/Getty Images Plus; Indeed; Kali9/E+; VTT Studio/iStock Editorial/Getty Images Plus; **U8:** Olesiabilkei/iStock/Getty Images Plus; Anton Kishinskiy/500px Prime; Zoonar RF/Getty Images Plus; Harry Engels/Getty Images Sport; Andresr/E+; Mint Images; Baramee Temboonkiat/iStock Editorial/Gett; Monkeybusinessimages/iStock/Getty Images Plus; **U9:** Jose Luis Pelaez Inc/DigitalVision; Kallista5/iStock/Getty Images Plus; Nortonrsx/iStock/Getty Images Plus; Kaarsten/iStock Editorial; David Gn Photography/Moment; **U10:** Flashpop/DigitalVision; Thomas Northcut/Photodisc; Nortonrsx/iStock/Getty Images Plus; B. BOISSONNET/BSIP/Corbis; SDI Productions/E+.

Cover photography by Drazen_/E+/Getty Images

Illustrations:
Kamae Design; David Semple.

Video stills:
Commissioned by Rob Maidment and Sharp Focus Productions.

Filming in King's College by kind permission of the Provost and Scholars of King's College, Cambridge.

Audio production by Graham Hart and by Creative Listening.

Typeset by QBS Learning.

Corpus
Development of this publication has made use of the Cambridge English Corpus (CEC). The CEC is a computer database of contemporary spoken and written English, which currently stands at over one billion words. It includes British English, American English and other varieties of English. It also includes the Cambridge Learner Corpus, developed in collaboration with the University of Cambridge ESOL Examinations. Cambridge University Press has built up the CEC to provide evidence about language use that helps us to produce better language teaching materials.

English Profile
This product is informed by English Vocabulary Profile, built as part of English Profile, a collaborative program designed to enhance the learning, teaching and assessment of English worldwide. Its main funding partners are Cambridge University Press and Cambridge Assessment English and its aim is to create a 'profile' for English, linked to the Common European Framework of Reference for Languages (CEFR). English Profile outcomes, such as the English Vocabulary Profile, will provide detailed information about the language that learners can be expected to demonstrate at each CEFR level, offering a clear benchmark for learners' proficiency. For more information, please visit www.englishprofile.org.

CALD
The Cambridge Advanced Learner's Dictionary is the world's most widely used dictionary for learners of English. Including all the words and phrases that learners are likely to come across, it also has easy to understand definitions and example sentences to show how the word is used in context. The Cambridge Advanced Learner's Dictionary is available online at dictionary.cambridge.org.

Shaftesbury Road, Cambridge CB2 8EA, United Kingdom

One Liberty Plaza, 20th Floor, New York, NY 10006, USA

477 Williamstown Road, Port Melbourne, VIC 3207, Australia

314–321, 3rd Floor, Plot 3, Splendor Forum, Jasola District Centre, New Delhi – 110025, India

103 Penang Road, #05–06/07, Visioncrest Commercial, Singapore 238467

Cambridge University Press & Assessment is a department of the University of Cambridge.

We share the University's mission to contribute to society through the pursuit of education, learning and research at the highest international levels of excellence.

www.cambridge.org
Information on this title: www.cambridge.org/9781108961592

First published 2022

20 19 18 17 16 15 14 13 12 11 10 9 8 7 6 5 4

Printed in Poland by Opolgraf

A catalogue record for this publication is available from the British Library

ISBN 978-1-108-95961-2 Advanced Student's Book with eBook
ISBN 978-1-108-96156-1 Advanced Student's Book with Digital Pack
ISBN 978-1-108-96159-2 Advanced Workbook with Answers
ISBN 978-1-108-96160-8 Advanced Workbook without Answers
ISBN 978-1-108-96157-8 Advanced Combo A with Digital Pack
ISBN 978-1-108-96158-5 Advanced Combo B with Digital Pack
ISBN 978-1-108-95550-8 Advanced Teacher's Book with Digital Pack
ISBN 978-1-108-95962-9 Advanced Presentation Plus

Additional resources for this publication at www.cambridge.org/empower

This page is intentionally left blank.